Flavors of Korea

DELICIOUS VEGETARIAN CUISINE

Deborah Coultrip-Davis
Young Sook Ramsay

Book Publishing Company
Summertown, Tennessee

Editor: Carol Wiley Lorente
Cover photograph: Dave Hawkins Photography Inc.
Cover design: Warren C. Jefferson & REKA Design
Cover photograph food stylist: Barb Bloomfield
Interior design: Warren C. Jefferson
Interior drawings: Jeannie Kahn

Pictured on cover, counterclockwise from upper left: Spinach Salad p.83, cabbage kimchi, Steamed Vegetables p. 88, Vegetable Bundles p. 94, Ginger Drink p. 173

Published in the United States of America by:

Book Publishing Co.
P.O. Box 99
Summertown, TN 38483
888-260-8458

09 08 07 06 05   6 5 4 3 2

ISBN 1-57067-053-6

Coultrip-Davis, Deborah,
      Flavors of Korea: delicious vegetarian cuisine / Deborah Coultrip-Davis & Young Sook Ramsay.
          p. cm.
      Includes index.
      ISBN 1-57067-053-6 (alk. paper)
      1. Vegetarian cookery. 2. Cookery, Korean. I. Ramsay, Young Sook, II. Title.
      TX837.C686   1998
      641.5'636'09519--dc21   98-18396   CIP

ACKNOWLEDGMENTS

To my mother, who taught me how to cook, to my father and mother, who introduced me to catering, to Young's mother and grandmother, who shared their recipes, and to my dear husband Jim, who supported me in every way, I thank you all.

Deb

Endure, Succeed, and Trust.
Thank you, Mother, Father, and Grandmother, for your love, inspiration, and prayers.

Young Sook

Table of Contents

Introduction

Spice and spunk, Korean cuisine. Synonymous words if ever there were any. Korean cooks have mastered the ability to turn plain-tasting vegetables into exciting, exhilarating dishes that will titilate and tantalize anyone's tastebuds. Using a variety of highly seasoned, fresh vegetables while utilizing low-fat, low-cholesterol methods of preparation, Korean food is the very type of diet health professionals are advocating today.

After nearly 15 years of sometimes quite bland vegetarian eating, I couldn't believe how delicious food could taste with the seasoned handling of an experienced Korean cook. Young Sook Ramsay introduced me to a whole new world of ethnic eating pleasure. The first Korean meal she made for me was truly memorable. The table was spread with colorful bowls of different Korean pickles, black beans, spicy egg strips, sesame spinach, fried tofu, seaweed squares, dips, and sauces. Plain white rice was served to temper the spiciness of some of the foods. Young had also prepared the paradoxical dish that inspired us to write this cookbook: Korean Cucumber Noodles, an exhilarating blend of opposites—hot red pepper and cool fresh cucumber—that delightfully complemented each other. At this meal, I was so impressed with what I then called a Korean buffet, I didn't realize until later that this was the typical way a Korean hostess would serve a meal—a myriad of savory dishes artfully displayed and temptingly delicious. This was and is classic Korean dining at its best.

As much as Korean cooking uses a wide assortment of vegetables, many of the traditional dishes also contain seafood, beef, chicken, or other meats. All of our recipes are vegetarian—none calls for meat, meat products, or meat broths, and most are vegan, devoid of all animal products. We have either eliminated or substituted for meat products and have exercised some creative ingenuity while maintaining the integrity of Korean cooking. We also have opted not to use monosodium glutamate in our recipes for health reasons. The spice and full flavors of the foods do not render it necessary.

Traditionally, Korean food contains one or more of the following ingredients: garlic, sesame oil or sesame seeds, or the indispensable red chili pepper in one form or another. This red chili pepper provides the punch in Korean cooking and is a staple in any Korean cupboard. It would behoove anyone trying to prepare these recipes to purchase the genuine red chili products. (Look for "gochu karu" on the package to ensure you're using authentic Korean seasoning.) The red pepper powder (cayenne) found on the condiment shelves of most supermarkets does not quite taste the same.

And that brings us to finding the ingredients for these recipes. Almost every food used in these dishes can be purchased in any well-stocked supermarket. A few items, such as gochujang (red pepper paste) and denjang paste (fermented soybean paste), can be purchased in either a supermarket or an Asian market. A large grocery store will often special order these products for its customers. Also, please see page 191 for a list of mail order companies from which one can order a varied selection of Asian foods and ingredients mentioned in our recipes.

Glossary

Bean Thread Noodles: Also called cellophane noodles because of their transparency, these Asian noodles are made from mung bean starch. They are sold dried and need no cooking—only a quick soak in water before using.

Buckwheat Noodles: Thin, tan-colored noodles made from black buckwheat seeds that have been ground into flour. This noodle has a discernible wheat flavor reminiscent of freshly baked bread.

Chinese Cabbage: Green, leafy, oblong cabbage frequently used in Korean pickled cabbage recipes.

Denjang Paste: Fermented soybean paste. It is used as a flavor enhancer and soup thickener.

Gochujang: Fermented hot pepper paste made from sweet rice, hot red pepper, soybeans, and salt. Gochujang provides the sizzle and red color in Korean cooking.

Kimchi: Probably the most renowned Korean dish, kimchi is a flavor-packed pickled food. Traditionally, herbs, spices, hot chili, fresh ginger, garlic, and salt were used as preservatives for foods the Koreans did not have available during the long winter months. The most recognized and pungent kimchi is the cabbage pickle, but kimchi can be made from a variety of different vegetables. There are probably more than 200 different kinds of kimchi.

Korean Radish: A whitish root vegetable from 3 to 10 inches long, used in some kimchis and side dishes. Purchase these vegetables with their leaves intact, since they are also edible and used in some recipes. The Japanese daikon radish is not as crunchy as the Korean radish but can be used interchangeably for the Korean radish in some recipes.

Korean Vermicelli: Very long, thin, greyish noodles made from sweet potatoes. Korean vermicelli is purchased dried. When cooked properly, these noodles are firm in texture yet supple and chewy. This is the type of noodle used in the popular Korean dish called Jap Chae.

Mandu Skins: Also called dumpling wrappers, these are round, paper-thin wrappings made from flour, eggs, and water and are dusted with cornstarch. Mandu skins can be found in either the refrigerator or freezer sections of Asian markets or any well-stocked grocery store.

Miyuk: See seaweed.

Mung Bean Curd: Pale, gelatinous blocks or cakes made from mung bean starch, measuring about 7 inches long by 4 inches wide by two inches thick. Like tofu, it does not have a strong flavor but readily absorbs the flavors of anything cooked with it.

Nori: See seaweed.

Pine Nuts: Nuts harvested from the pine cones of a variety of pine trees and one of the traditional ingredients in pesto. Available in the produce section of most supermarkets.

Red Chili Pepper: Several forms of red pepper are used in Korean cooking, including flakes, powder, and threads. Flakes are the result of coarsely crushing seeded and dried red chili peppers; they are tiny, visible framents of red pepper. Red pepper powder is the finely ground, dried husk of the chili pepper; this is the red pepper powder used in gochujang and in many of the kimchi recipes. Red pepper threads are long, thin strings of hot red chilis that have been dried; they are used for decorative purposes as well as for providing a very mild bite to the food.

Rice Cakes: Korean rice cakes are not the same as the crunchy, round Japanese crackers popular in this country. They are usually long, white, and cylindrical (although they come in different shapes) and are made from glutinous rice, water, and salt. They are sold in Asian markets, usually in packages of two or three fresh rice cakes per package. Rice cakes are chewy and mild tasting, therefore a complementary adjunct to spicier foods.

Rice Flour: White, starchy flour made from rice and used as a thickening agent in some kimchis.

Rice Vinegar: Used in cooking and salads when a slightly sweeter, more delicately flavored vinegar is desired.

Seaweed: Seaweed provides color, flavor, protein, and vitamins to Korean cooking. Different types of seaweed are used for different purposes. Kelp is a dried seaweed that expands when submerged in water; it is used in soups. Laver or nori is a dark greenish-brown, almost black seaweed sold in thin 6-by 8-inch pieces and used in recipes such as toasted seaweed squares and Kim Bap (Seaweed Rice Rolls). Miyuk is a dark-brown seaweed used in soups and broths.

Sesame Seeds: Sesame seeds are available toasted or raw and are used as flavorings and/or garnishes.

Sesame Oil: With its alluring, nutty flavor, sesame oil is used in sauces and side dishes to enhance natural flavors. Sesame chili oil imparts both a subtle sesame flavor along with an extra red pepper zing. There is a tempura sesame oil on the market that can be substituted for any vegetable oil to give fried foods a sesame flavor, or you can add a few drops of sesame oil to vegetable oil and fry the foods as usual.

Tofu: Called tubu, bean curd, or soybean curd in Korea, tofu was originally invented by the Chinese, but other Asian countries soon discovered its versatility and healthful qualities. Tofu is a high-protein, no-cholesterol, low-sodium, low-calorie product made from soymilk. Tofu can be purchased in either soft or firm blocks. Koreans use both types—it seems to depend on personal preference. Because of its ability to readily absorb seasonings, it is an almost magical ingredient that allows those spirited Korean seasonings to come alive.

Soups & Stews

KUK & JUK

K orean soups are delicious creations served hot or cold, mild or spicy. Whatever the palate desires, there is sure to be a soup in this chapter to satisfy. For a quick, easy, light appetizer, for example, try Radish Soup (Moo Kuk). If your taste leans more towards thick and hearty, try any of the soups or stews requiring denjang paste. This tasty flavor enhancer works as a versatile soup base; it can be added to just about any vegetable or vegetable combination for a ready-in-minutes soup.

Feeling under the weather? Try a Korean (and vegetarian) version of chicken soup: Kimchi Soup (Kimchi Kuk). The spice and fire in this creation will have you feeling better before you can put your spoon down. Or would you like something refreshingly cool on a hot summer day? Cold Noodle Soup (Nang Kuksu) is just the answer—buckwheat noodles in a savory broth, garnished with cucumbers, pears, and sliced eggs. Whatever one's taste, there is enough variety in Korean soups to satisfy even the most discriminating diner.

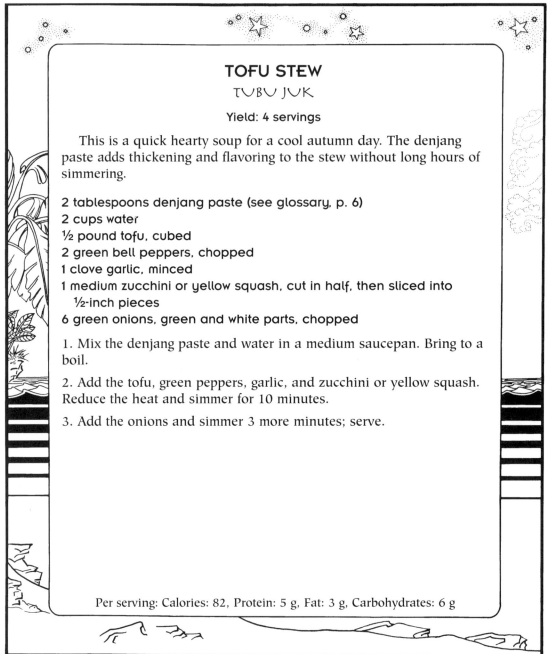

TOFU STEW
TUBU JUK

Yield: 4 servings

This is a quick hearty soup for a cool autumn day. The denjang paste adds thickening and flavoring to the stew without long hours of simmering.

2 tablespoons denjang paste (see glossary, p. 6)
2 cups water
½ pound tofu, cubed
2 green bell peppers, chopped
1 clove garlic, minced
1 medium zucchini or yellow squash, cut in half, then sliced into
    ½-inch pieces
6 green onions, green and white parts, chopped

1. Mix the denjang paste and water in a medium saucepan. Bring to a boil.

2. Add the tofu, green peppers, garlic, and zucchini or yellow squash. Reduce the heat and simmer for 10 minutes.

3. Add the onions and simmer 3 more minutes; serve.

Per serving: Calories: 82, Protein: 5 g, Fat: 3 g, Carbohydrates: 6 g

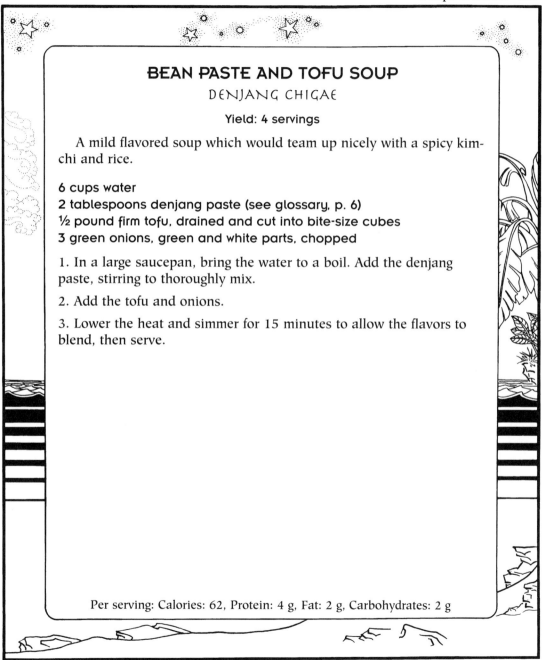

BEAN PASTE AND TOFU SOUP

DENJANG CHIGAE

Yield: 4 servings

A mild flavored soup which would team up nicely with a spicy kimchi and rice.

6 cups water
2 tablespoons denjang paste (see glossary, p. 6)
½ pound firm tofu, drained and cut into bite-size cubes
3 green onions, green and white parts, chopped

1. In a large saucepan, bring the water to a boil. Add the denjang paste, stirring to thoroughly mix.

2. Add the tofu and onions.

3. Lower the heat and simmer for 15 minutes to allow the flavors to blend, then serve.

Per serving: Calories: 62, Protein: 4 g, Fat: 2 g, Carbohydrates: 2 g

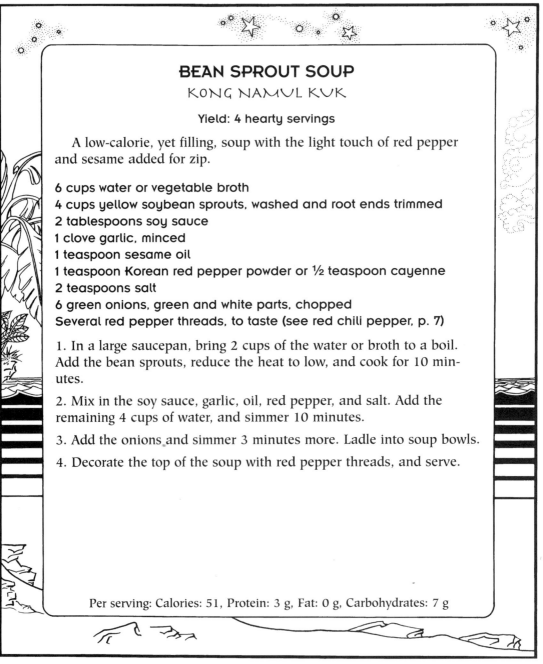

BEAN SPROUT SOUP

KONG NAMUL KUK

Yield: 4 hearty servings

A low-calorie, yet filling, soup with the light touch of red pepper and sesame added for zip.

6 cups water or vegetable broth
4 cups yellow soybean sprouts, washed and root ends trimmed
2 tablespoons soy sauce
1 clove garlic, minced
1 teaspoon sesame oil
1 teaspoon Korean red pepper powder or ½ teaspoon cayenne
2 teaspoons salt
6 green onions, green and white parts, chopped
Several red pepper threads, to taste (see red chili pepper, p. 7)

1. In a large saucepan, bring 2 cups of the water or broth to a boil. Add the bean sprouts, reduce the heat to low, and cook for 10 minutes.

2. Mix in the soy sauce, garlic, oil, red pepper, and salt. Add the remaining 4 cups of water, and simmer 10 minutes.

3. Add the onions and simmer 3 minutes more. Ladle into soup bowls.

4. Decorate the top of the soup with red pepper threads, and serve.

Per serving: Calories: 51, Protein: 3 g, Fat: 0 g, Carbohydrates: 7 g

CARROT SOUP

DANGOON KUK

Yield: 4 servings

3 large carrots, diced
1 cup shredded Chinese cabbage
5 cups water
1 clove garlic, minced
4 green onions, green and white parts, chopped
1½ tablespoons denjang paste (see glossary, p. 6)
Salt and pepper, to taste

1. In a medium saucepan, add the carrots, cabbage, and water. Bring to a boil and simmer until the carrots and cabbage are tender, about 10 minutes.

2. Add the garlic, green onions, and denjang paste. Stir until the denjang paste dissolves. Add salt and pepper and serve.

Per serving: Calories: 42, Protein: 1 g, Fat: 0 g, Carbohydrates: 7 g

COLD NOODLE SOUP
NANG KUKSU

Yield: 4 servings

If soup can be called serene, then Nang Kuksu is serene. Islands of tan buckwheat noodles artfully adorned with garnish rest quitely in a pool of delicately spiced broth. After appreciating the visual appeal of Nang Kuksu, enliven the picture with the mustard and pepper sauces, and let your taste buds appreciate this wonderful dish too.

This dish also introduces us to Korean pears. Korean pears differ from American pears in that they are round, very firm, and not as sweet, but they are quite flavorful. Look for Korean pears in the exotic produce section of most large supermarkets or in Asian markets. Asian pears, which look and taste similar to Korean pears, may be substituted.

6 cups vegetable broth
2 inches of fresh ginger root, peeled and sliced
2 cups kimchi juice (see glossary, p. 6)
½ teaspoon salt
1 tablespoon vinegar
1 tablespoon sugar
½ pound buckwheat noodles (see glossary, p. 6)

Garnishes:
1 small seedless cucumber, ends trimmed, cut in half lengthwise and
    then thinly sliced crosswise
½ teaspoon salt
1 teaspoon vegetable oil plus a few drops of sesame oil (see glos-
    sary, p. 9)
½ Korean pear, peeled and shredded
2 hard-boiled eggs, sliced lengthwise

Pepper Sauce:
2 teaspoons freshly ground black pepper
2 teaspoons sesame oil
1 clove garlic, crushed
¼ teaspoon salt

Mustard Sauce:
2 tablespoons dry mustard
2 tablespoons water

1. In a large saucepan, bring the vegetable broth, ginger, kimchi juice, salt, vinegar, and sugar to a boil. Reduce the heat and simmer for 30 minutes. Remove the ginger from the broth, and discard; set the broth aside to cool.

2. In a large pot, cook the noodles in boiling water until al dente, about 2 to 3 minutes. Drain and rinse under cold water. Set aside.

3. In a small bowl, sprinkle the cucumber slices with salt, and let stand for 10 minutes. Squeeze the cucumbers with your hands to remove excess water.

4. In a small skillet over medium heat, add the oil and fry the cucumber slices for 1 minute. Transfer them to a serving dish, and set aside.

5. Divide the noodles among four deep soup bowls. Arrange the slices of cucumber, pear, and egg on top of the noodles. Ladle about 2 cups of the cold broth over the noodles.

6. To make the sauces, mix the ingredients in small bowls or cups.

7. Serve the soup with the sauces on the side.

Tip: The noodles may be snipped with cooking shears to a suitable eating length.

Per serving: Calories: 328, Protein: 12 g, Fat: 5 g, Carbohydrates: 56 g

DUMPLING SOUP

MANDU KUK

Yield: 4 servings

Plump dumplings and chewy rice cake slices combine to make this an interesting experience in taste and texture.

6 cups water
One 8-inch rice cake, thinly sliced on the diagonal (see glossary, p. 8)
1 teaspoon salt
¼ teaspoon black pepper
2 tablespoons soy sauce, or to taste
12 Vegetable Dumplings (p. 146-47)
4 green onions, green and white parts, chopped
1 egg, beaten

Garnish: 1 sheet nori, toasted and crumbled (see seaweed, p. 8, and hint below)

1. In a large saucepan or Dutch oven, bring the water, rice cake slices, salt, pepper, and soy sauce to a boil. Reduce the heat to low, and simmer for 20 minutes.

2. Add the vegetable dumplings and onions. Simmer 15 minutes more.

3. Add the beaten egg. Simmer 2 minutes longer.

4. Place in four individual bowls. Garnish with the crumbled nori, and serve warm.

Helpful hint: Nori is a dark, greenish-brown seaweed sold in thin, 6- by 8-inch sheets. To toast nori, brush it lightly with vegetable or sesame oil. Heat a large, nonstick pan or skillet over medium heat. Place the nori sheets in the pan for a few seconds on each side.

Per serving: Calories: 121, Protein: 5 g, Fat: 2 g, Carbohydrates: 4 g

EGGPLANT STEW

KAJI JUK

Yield: 4 servings

½ tablespoon vegetable oil
2 Japanese eggplants, cut into bite-size cubes
4 green onions, green and white parts, chopped
2 cloves garlic, minced
4 cups hot water
2 tablespoons denjang paste (see glossary, p. 6)
Salt and pepper, to taste

1. In a large saucepan or Dutch oven, heat the oil over medium-high heat. Fry the eggplant until it is slightly brown and limp, about 4 minutes.

2. Add the onions and garlic, and cook 1 minute.

3. Add the water and denjang paste. Bring to a boil, stirring constantly, until the denjang paste is dissolved. Reduce the heat to a simmer, and cook 5 minutes longer to allow the flavors to blend. Add salt and pepper to taste. Serve warm.

Per serving: Calories: 48, Protein: 0 g, Fat: 2 g, Carbohydrates: 4 g

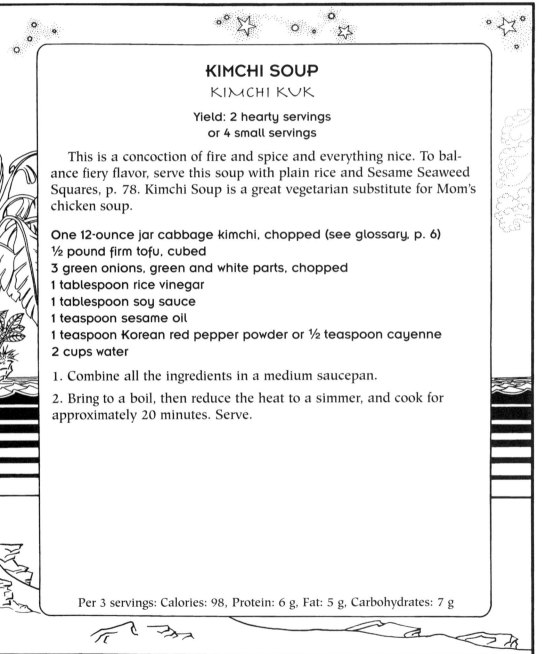

KIMCHI SOUP
KIMCHI KUK

**Yield: 2 hearty servings
or 4 small servings**

This is a concoction of fire and spice and everything nice. To balance fiery flavor, serve this soup with plain rice and Sesame Seaweed Squares, p. 78. Kimchi Soup is a great vegetarian substitute for Mom's chicken soup.

One 12-ounce jar cabbage kimchi, chopped (see glossary, p. 6)
½ pound firm tofu, cubed
3 green onions, green and white parts, chopped
1 tablespoon rice vinegar
1 tablespoon soy sauce
1 teaspoon sesame oil
1 teaspoon Korean red pepper powder or ½ teaspoon cayenne
2 cups water

1. Combine all the ingredients in a medium saucepan.

2. Bring to a boil, then reduce the heat to a simmer, and cook for approximately 20 minutes. Serve.

Per 3 servings: Calories: 98, Protein: 6 g, Fat: 5 g, Carbohydrates: 7 g

MUSHROOM SOUP

BOSOT KUK

Yield: 4 servings

1½ teaspoons vegetable oil
½ pound fresh button mushrooms, cleaned and thinly sliced
4 green onions, green and white parts, chopped
3 cloves garlic, minced
4 cups water
2½ tablespoons denjang paste (see glossary, p. 6)

1. In a medium skillet, heat the oil over medium-high heat. Add the mushrooms and sauté until lightly brown and slightly limp, about 3 minutes.

2. Add the onions and garlic, and sauté 1 minute.

3. In a large saucepan, heat the water and denjang paste to boiling, stirring constantly, until the denjang paste is dissolved. Add the mushroom mixture. Reduce the heat and simmer 4 minutes. Serve warm.

Per serving: Calories: 55, Protein: 1 g, Fat: 2 g, Carbohydrates: 4 g

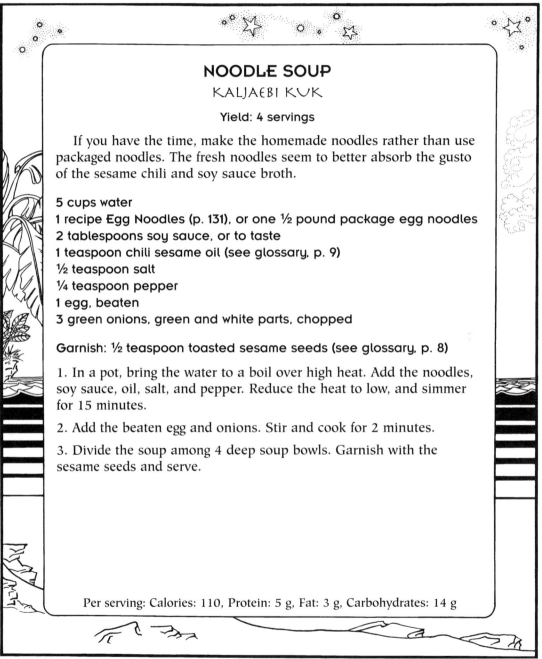

NOODLE SOUP

KALJAEBI KUK

Yield: 4 servings

If you have the time, make the homemade noodles rather than use packaged noodles. The fresh noodles seem to better absorb the gusto of the sesame chili and soy sauce broth.

5 cups water
1 recipe Egg Noodles (p. 131), or one ½ pound package egg noodles
2 tablespoons soy sauce, or to taste
1 teaspoon chili sesame oil (see glossary, p. 9)
½ teaspoon salt
¼ teaspoon pepper
1 egg, beaten
3 green onions, green and white parts, chopped

Garnish: ½ teaspoon toasted sesame seeds (see glossary, p. 8)

1. In a pot, bring the water to a boil over high heat. Add the noodles, soy sauce, oil, salt, and pepper. Reduce the heat to low, and simmer for 15 minutes.

2. Add the beaten egg and onions. Stir and cook for 2 minutes.

3. Divide the soup among 4 deep soup bowls. Garnish with the sesame seeds and serve.

Per serving: Calories: 110, Protein: 5 g, Fat: 3 g, Carbohydrates: 14 g

POTATO LEEK SOUP

KAMJA PUCHU KUK

Yield: 4 servings

2 teaspoons vegetable oil
2 small leeks, green and white parts, thinly sliced
5 cups water
2 tablespoons denjang paste (see glossary, p. 6)
2 large potatoes (preferably red, but any type works well), cooked,
   peeled, and cut into bite-size cubes

1. In a medium skillet, heat the oil over medium-high heat. Add the leeks and fry until golden brown and limp, about 2 minutes. Remove from the heat and set aside.

2. In a large saucepan or pot, heat the water and denjang paste to a boil over high heat, stirring constantly, until the denjang paste is dissolved.

3. Add the potatoes and leeks. Simmer 5 minutes and serve.

Per serving: Calories: 134, Protein: 1 g, Fat: 2 g, Carbohydrates: 23 g

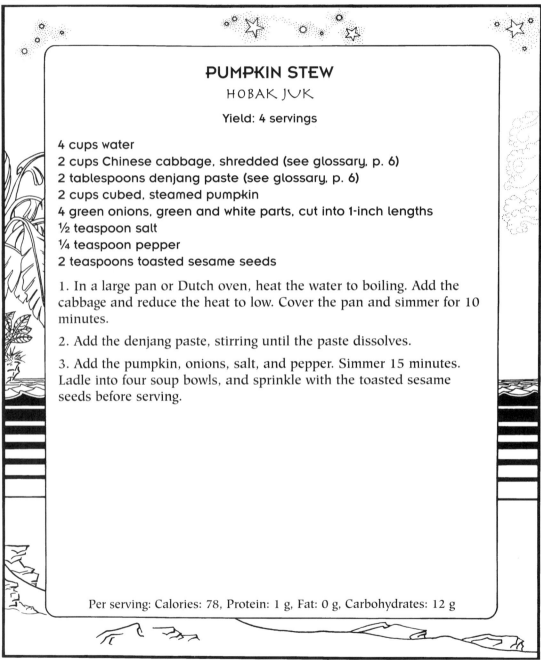

PUMPKIN STEW

HOBAK JUK

Yield: 4 servings

4 cups water
2 cups Chinese cabbage, shredded (see glossary, p. 6)
2 tablespoons denjang paste (see glossary, p. 6)
2 cups cubed, steamed pumpkin
4 green onions, green and white parts, cut into 1-inch lengths
½ teaspoon salt
¼ teaspoon pepper
2 teaspoons toasted sesame seeds

1. In a large pan or Dutch oven, heat the water to boiling. Add the cabbage and reduce the heat to low. Cover the pan and simmer for 10 minutes.

2. Add the denjang paste, stirring until the paste dissolves.

3. Add the pumpkin, onions, salt, and pepper. Simmer 15 minutes. Ladle into four soup bowls, and sprinkle with the toasted sesame seeds before serving.

Per serving: Calories: 78, Protein: 1 g, Fat: 0 g, Carbohydrates: 12 g

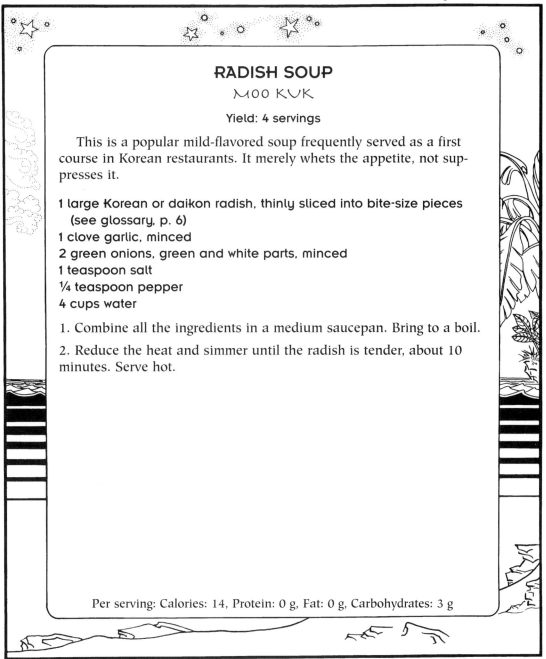

RADISH SOUP

MOO KUK

Yield: 4 servings

This is a popular mild-flavored soup frequently served as a first course in Korean restaurants. It merely whets the appetite, not suppresses it.

1 large Korean or daikon radish, thinly sliced into bite-size pieces (see glossary, p. 6)
1 clove garlic, minced
2 green onions, green and white parts, minced
1 teaspoon salt
¼ teaspoon pepper
4 cups water

1. Combine all the ingredients in a medium saucepan. Bring to a boil.

2. Reduce the heat and simmer until the radish is tender, about 10 minutes. Serve hot.

Per serving: Calories: 14, Protein: 0 g, Fat: 0 g, Carbohydrates: 3 g

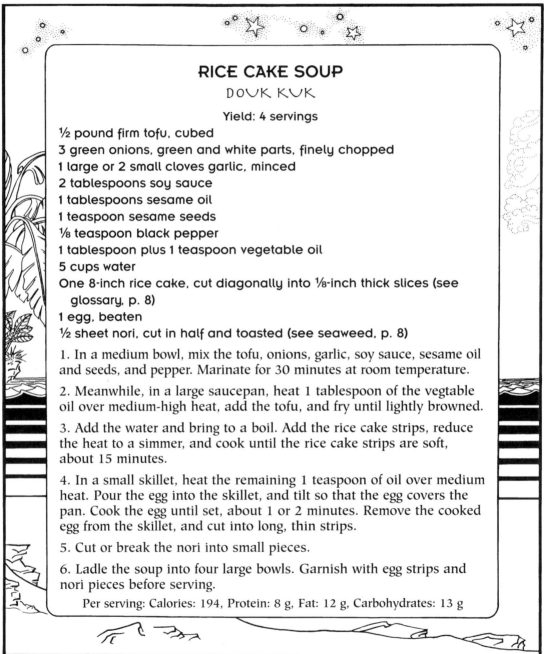

RICE CAKE SOUP

DOUK KUK

Yield: 4 servings

½ pound firm tofu, cubed
3 green onions, green and white parts, finely chopped
1 large or 2 small cloves garlic, minced
2 tablespoons soy sauce
1 tablespoons sesame oil
1 teaspoon sesame seeds
⅛ teaspoon black pepper
1 tablespoon plus 1 teaspoon vegetable oil
5 cups water
One 8-inch rice cake, cut diagonally into ⅛-inch thick slices (see
    glossary, p. 8)
1 egg, beaten
½ sheet nori, cut in half and toasted (see seaweed, p. 8)

1. In a medium bowl, mix the tofu, onions, garlic, soy sauce, sesame oil
and seeds, and pepper. Marinate for 30 minutes at room temperature.

2. Meanwhile, in a large saucepan, heat 1 tablespoon of the vegtable
oil over medium-high heat, add the tofu, and fry until lightly browned.

3. Add the water and bring to a boil. Add the rice cake strips, reduce
the heat to a simmer, and cook until the rice cake strips are soft,
about 15 minutes.

4. In a small skillet, heat the remaining 1 teaspoon of oil over medium
heat. Pour the egg into the skillet, and tilt so that the egg covers the
pan. Cook the egg until set, about 1 or 2 minutes. Remove the cooked
egg from the skillet, and cut into long, thin strips.

5. Cut or break the nori into small pieces.

6. Ladle the soup into four large bowls. Garnish with egg strips and
nori pieces before serving.

Per serving: Calories: 194, Protein: 8 g, Fat: 12 g, Carbohydrates: 13 g

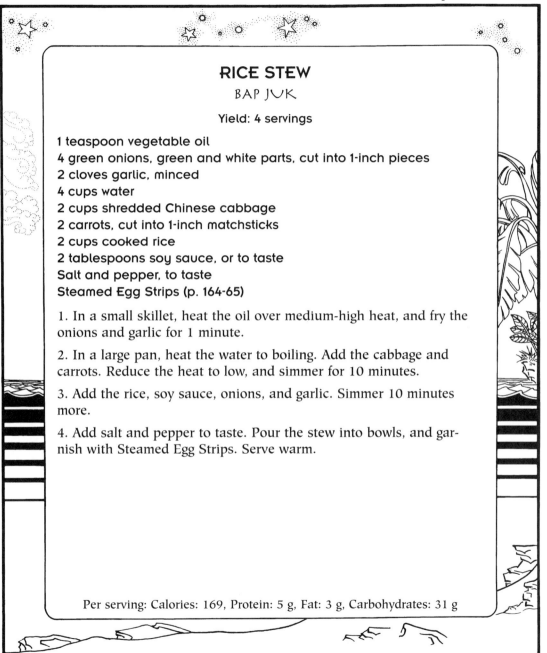

RICE STEW

BAP JUK

Yield: 4 servings

1 teaspoon vegetable oil
4 green onions, green and white parts, cut into 1-inch pieces
2 cloves garlic, minced
4 cups water
2 cups shredded Chinese cabbage
2 carrots, cut into 1-inch matchsticks
2 cups cooked rice
2 tablespoons soy sauce, or to taste
Salt and pepper, to taste
Steamed Egg Strips (p. 164-65)

1. In a small skillet, heat the oil over medium-high heat, and fry the onions and garlic for 1 minute.

2. In a large pan, heat the water to boiling. Add the cabbage and carrots. Reduce the heat to low, and simmer for 10 minutes.

3. Add the rice, soy sauce, onions, and garlic. Simmer 10 minutes more.

4. Add salt and pepper to taste. Pour the stew into bowls, and garnish with Steamed Egg Strips. Serve warm.

Per serving: Calories: 169, Protein: 5 g, Fat: 3 g, Carbohydrates: 31 g

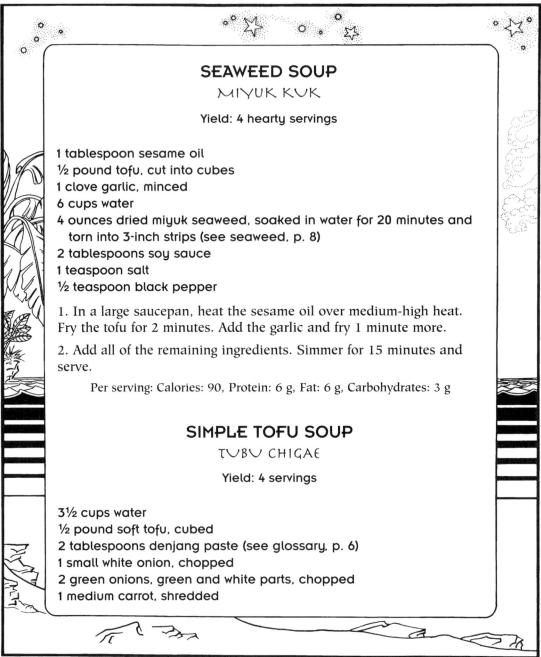

SEAWEED SOUP
MIYUK KUK

Yield: 4 hearty servings

1 tablespoon sesame oil
½ pound tofu, cut into cubes
1 clove garlic, minced
6 cups water
4 ounces dried miyuk seaweed, soaked in water for 20 minutes and
   torn into 3-inch strips (see seaweed, p. 8)
2 tablespoons soy sauce
1 teaspoon salt
½ teaspoon black pepper

1. In a large saucepan, heat the sesame oil over medium-high heat. Fry the tofu for 2 minutes. Add the garlic and fry 1 minute more.

2. Add all of the remaining ingredients. Simmer for 15 minutes and serve.

Per serving: Calories: 90, Protein: 6 g, Fat: 6 g, Carbohydrates: 3 g

SIMPLE TOFU SOUP
TUBU CHIGAE

Yield: 4 servings

3½ cups water
½ pound soft tofu, cubed
2 tablespoons denjang paste (see glossary, p. 6)
1 small white onion, chopped
2 green onions, green and white parts, chopped
1 medium carrot, shredded

½ teaspoon salt
¼ teaspoon black pepper

1. In a medium pan, bring the water to a boil over high heat.

2. Add all of the remaining ingredients. Cover and simmer 15 minutes before serving.

> Per serving: Calories: 76, Protein: 4 g, Fat: 3 g, Carbohydrates: 5 g

SPINACH SOUP

SIKUMCHI KUK

Yield: 5 hearty servings

6 cups water
2 tablespoons denjang paste (see glossary, p. 6)
4 cups fresh spinach leaves, chopped, or 10 ounces frozen, chopped
  spinach, thawed, squeezed, and drained
½ pound tofu, cubed
1 tablespoon soy sauce
1 clove garlic, minced
½ teaspoon sesame oil
3 green onions, green and white parts, finely chopped
1 teaspoon sesame seeds
Black pepper, to taste

1. In a large saucepan, bring the water and denjang paste to a boil, stirring until the denjang paste has dissolved.

2. Add the spinach, tofu, soy sauce, garlic, and oil. Simmer 3 minutes.

3. Add the onions and sesame seeds, and simmer 2 minutes more.

4. Add black pepper to taste, and serve.

> Per serving: Calories: 69, Protein: 4 g, Fat: 2 g, Carbohydrates: 3 g

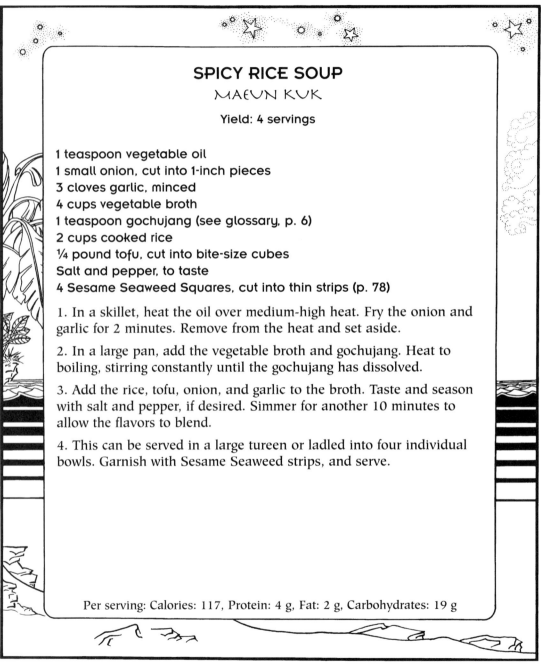

SPICY RICE SOUP

MAEUN KUK

Yield: 4 servings

1 teaspoon vegetable oil
1 small onion, cut into 1-inch pieces
3 cloves garlic, minced
4 cups vegetable broth
1 teaspoon gochujang (see glossary, p. 6)
2 cups cooked rice
¼ pound tofu, cut into bite-size cubes
Salt and pepper, to taste
4 Sesame Seaweed Squares, cut into thin strips (p. 78)

1. In a skillet, heat the oil over medium-high heat. Fry the onion and garlic for 2 minutes. Remove from the heat and set aside.

2. In a large pan, add the vegetable broth and gochujang. Heat to boiling, stirring constantly until the gochujang has dissolved.

3. Add the rice, tofu, onion, and garlic to the broth. Taste and season with salt and pepper, if desired. Simmer for another 10 minutes to allow the flavors to blend.

4. This can be served in a large tureen or ladled into four individual bowls. Garnish with Sesame Seaweed strips, and serve.

Per serving: Calories: 117, Protein: 4 g, Fat: 2 g, Carbohydrates: 19 g

SQUASH SOUP

HOBAK KUK

Yield: 4 hearty servings

2 teaspoons vegetable oil

1 small yellow squash, cut in half lengthwise and thinly sliced crosswise

1 small zucchini, cut lengthwise and thinly sliced crosswise

1 onion, cut into 1-inch pieces

2 cloves garlic, minced

1 green bell pepper, seeded and cut into 1-inch long matchsticks

6 cups water

3 tablespoons denjang paste (see glossary, p. 6)

8 red chili threads, broken into smaller pieces (see red chili pepper,
   p. 7)

2 teaspoons toasted sesame seeds

1. In a skillet, heat the oil over medium-high heat. Add the squash, zucchini, onion, garlic, and green pepper. Stir-fry for 3 minutes. Remove from the heat and set aside.

2. In a large pan or Dutch oven, add the water and denjang paste. Heat to boiling, stirring constantly, until the denjang paste has dissolved.

3. Add the stir-fried vegetables to the boiling broth, and reduce the heat to low. Simmer for 10 minutes.

4. This soup can be served in a large tureen or ladled into individual bowls. Garnish with red chili threads and toasted sesame seeds before serving.

Helpful hint: To toast sesame seeds, heat a nonstick skillet over medium heat. Add the sesame seeds to the skillet, and stir continuously. The seeds will jump and pop, but continue cooking until they are golden brown, about 5 minutes. Remove the toasted seeds from the pan immediately to prevent burning; cool. Store in a jar in a cool, dry place.

Per serving: Calories: 82, Protein: 1 g, Fat: 3 g, Carbohydrates: 7 g

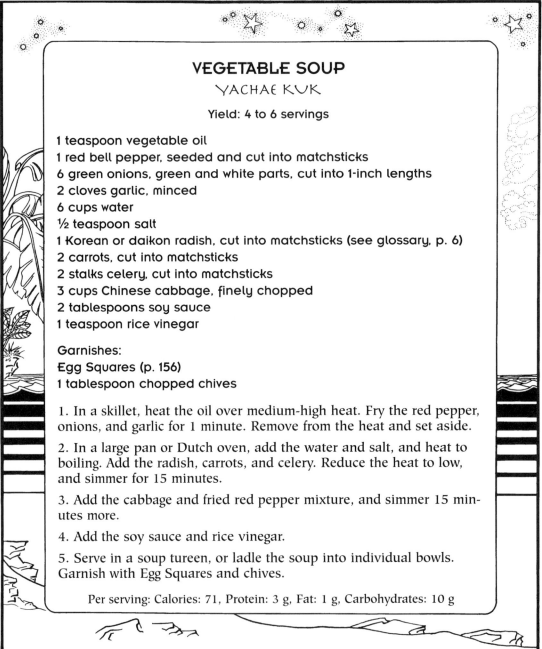

VEGETABLE SOUP
YACHAE KUK

Yield: 4 to 6 servings

1 teaspoon vegetable oil
1 red bell pepper, seeded and cut into matchsticks
6 green onions, green and white parts, cut into 1-inch lengths
2 cloves garlic, minced
6 cups water
½ teaspoon salt
1 Korean or daikon radish, cut into matchsticks (see glossary, p. 6)
2 carrots, cut into matchsticks
2 stalks celery, cut into matchsticks
3 cups Chinese cabbage, finely chopped
2 tablespoons soy sauce
1 teaspoon rice vinegar

Garnishes:
Egg Squares (p. 156)
1 tablespoon chopped chives

1. In a skillet, heat the oil over medium-high heat. Fry the red pepper, onions, and garlic for 1 minute. Remove from the heat and set aside.

2. In a large pan or Dutch oven, add the water and salt, and heat to boiling. Add the radish, carrots, and celery. Reduce the heat to low, and simmer for 15 minutes.

3. Add the cabbage and fried red pepper mixture, and simmer 15 minutes more.

4. Add the soy sauce and rice vinegar.

5. Serve in a soup tureen, or ladle the soup into individual bowls. Garnish with Egg Squares and chives.

Per serving: Calories: 71, Protein: 3 g, Fat: 1 g, Carbohydrates: 10 g

Korean Pickles

KIMCHI

Kimchi is probably one of the most notable and popular of all the Korean side dishes. Although Asian cabbage (also called Chinese or napa cabbage) is the one vegetable usually associated with kimchi, ingenious Korean cooks have created hundreds of different kimchi recipes using the myriad seasonal vegetables available in different regions of their country.

However the main vegetable ingredients may vary, most kimchi recipes have several common ingredients. Salt is used as the preserving agent, accompanied by red pepper, garlic, and onion, which enhance the natural vegetable flavors. Ginger root is another favorite addition. Fresh vegetables are always used, and some recipes call for anchovy paste, pickled shrimp or raw fish, or seafood. Fortunately, there are plenty of vegetarian kimchi recipes from which to choose.

Originally, making kimchi was a way to preserve vegetables to be used as a food source during the long winter months. The kimchi was prepared in the autumn, placed in large, black, earthenware pots called jang dok, and buried in the ground for winter storage. Young has regaled me with stories of her youth, when she would arrive home from school and her mother's kitchen would be filled with Korean women in a communal effort of cutting, chopping, and mixing the vegetables and spices, then storing the concoctions in the large black pots for the long, cool fermentation and transformation into a tasty winter dish. All Korean families looked forward to sampling the fiery results of the kimchi makers' efforts.

Don't let the length of time it takes the kimchi to ripen deter you from trying these recipes. There are many fresh kimchis—such as Cucumber Pickle (Oi Kimchi)—which take very little time and effort to prepare. A general rule for the length of time before the kimchi is ready to eat is: "More salt, more wait; less salt, less wait." There might be a detectable taste difference between the fresh and long-term (several days or months) kimchi. The flavors in the long-term kimchi are sometimes more powerful. This is because the salt draws liquid from the vegetables which then mixes with the garlic, onion, and red pepper. The longer time gives these liquids more time to ferment and creates the delectable sauce for which kimchi is known. But whether trying the quick or long-term kimchi versions, jaded tastebuds will definitely perk up.

There is one very important rule to remember when storing kimchi: If a recipe calls for letting the kimchi mature or ripen in a cool room, make sure that the room is cool enough. If the kimchi gets too warm, it will spoil. A good storage place would be in a cool, dry basement. Of course, you can try the Korean way and bury it in a cool spot deep underground. If neither of these options appeals to you, just let the kimchi ripen in the refrigerator. To prevent the pungent kimchi odor from permeating other refrigerator foods, place the kimchi jar inside of a large plastic bag, and enclose the bag. Although kimchi has a deliciously piquant taste and smell, that coconut cream pie sitting next to the jar in the refrigerator will not taste quite the same with a kimchi tang to it!

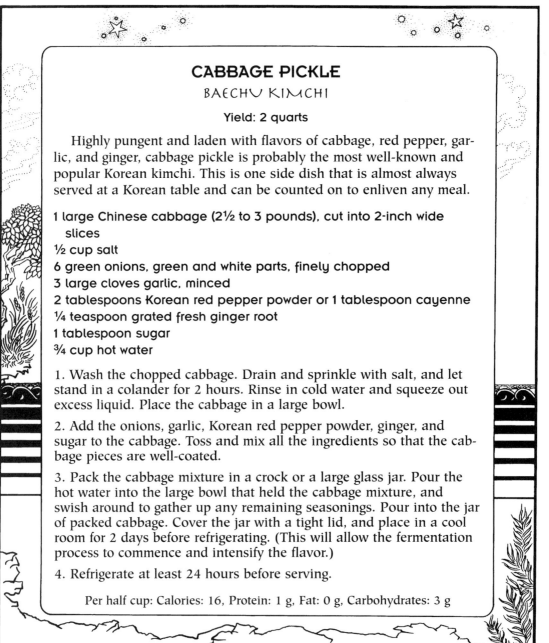

CABBAGE PICKLE

BAECHU KIMCHI

Yield: 2 quarts

Highly pungent and laden with flavors of cabbage, red pepper, garlic, and ginger, cabbage pickle is probably the most well-known and popular Korean kimchi. This is one side dish that is almost always served at a Korean table and can be counted on to enliven any meal.

1 large Chinese cabbage (2½ to 3 pounds), cut into 2-inch wide slices
½ cup salt
6 green onions, green and white parts, finely chopped
3 large cloves garlic, minced
2 tablespoons Korean red pepper powder or 1 tablespoon cayenne
¼ teaspoon grated fresh ginger root
1 tablespoon sugar
¾ cup hot water

1. Wash the chopped cabbage. Drain and sprinkle with salt, and let stand in a colander for 2 hours. Rinse in cold water and squeeze out excess liquid. Place the cabbage in a large bowl.

2. Add the onions, garlic, Korean red pepper powder, ginger, and sugar to the cabbage. Toss and mix all the ingredients so that the cabbage pieces are well-coated.

3. Pack the cabbage mixture in a crock or a large glass jar. Pour the hot water into the large bowl that held the cabbage mixture, and swish around to gather up any remaining seasonings. Pour into the jar of packed cabbage. Cover the jar with a tight lid, and place in a cool room for 2 days before refrigerating. (This will allow the fermentation process to commence and intensify the flavor.)

4. Refrigerate at least 24 hours before serving.

Per half cup: Calories: 16, Protein: 1 g, Fat: 0 g, Carbohydrates: 3 g

CABBAGE RADISH PICKLE
BAECHU MOO KIMCHI

Yield: 2 quarts

1 pound Korean or daikon radish, cut into matchsticks (see glossary, p. 6)
2 pounds Chinese cabbage, cut lengthwise and crosswise into 2-inch pieces
3 tablespoons salt dissolved in ½ gallon cold water

Seasonings:
5 green onions, green and white parts, minced
2 cloves garlic, minced
½ teaspoon grated fresh ginger root
2 tablespoons Korean red pepper powder or 1 tablespoon cayenne
3 tablespoons hot water

1. Place the radish strips on the bottom of a large bowl, and layer the cabbage on top. Pour the salt water over the vegetables. Place a heavy plate on top of the cabbage and radish to keep the vegetables under the brine. Let stand for 8 hours or overnight.

2. Drain the cabbage and radish, discarding the brine. Rinse in clear water, drain, and squeeze out any remaining liquid.

3. In a small bowl, mix the seasonings together and sprinkle over the vegetables. Toss the mixture until the seasonings have thoroughly coated the cabbage and radish.

4. Place in a 2-quart plastic or glass container. Pour the hot water over the vegetables and tightly seal. Place in a cool room for 2 or 3 days before serving to develop that disinctive kimchi flavor.

Per half cup: Calories: 15, Protein: 1 g, Fat: 0 g, Carbohydrates: 3 g

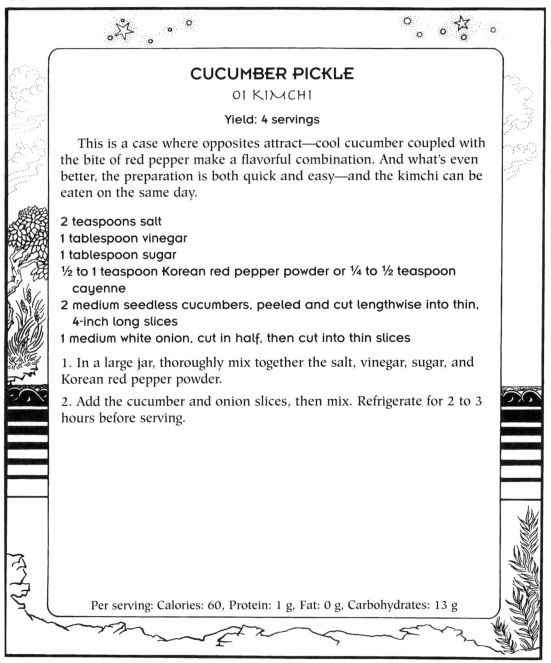

CUCUMBER PICKLE

OI KIMCHI

Yield: 4 servings

This is a case where opposites attract—cool cucumber coupled with the bite of red pepper make a flavorful combination. And what's even better, the preparation is both quick and easy—and the kimchi can be eaten on the same day.

2 teaspoons salt
1 tablespoon vinegar
1 tablespoon sugar
½ to 1 teaspoon Korean red pepper powder or ¼ to ½ teaspoon
   cayenne
2 medium seedless cucumbers, peeled and cut lengthwise into thin,
   4-inch long slices
1 medium white onion, cut in half, then cut into thin slices

1. In a large jar, thoroughly mix together the salt, vinegar, sugar, and Korean red pepper powder.

2. Add the cucumber and onion slices, then mix. Refrigerate for 2 to 3 hours before serving.

Per serving: Calories: 60, Protein: 1 g, Fat: 0 g, Carbohydrates: 13 g

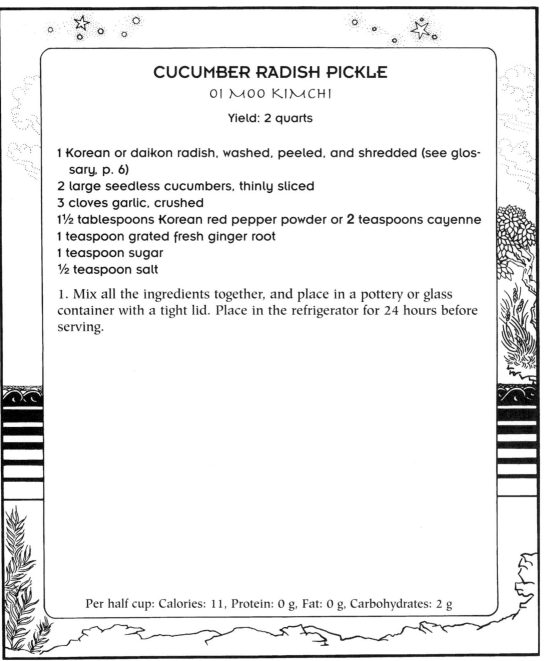

CUCUMBER RADISH PICKLE

OI MOO KIMCHI

Yield: 2 quarts

1 Korean or daikon radish, washed, peeled, and shredded (see glossary, p. 6)
2 large seedless cucumbers, thinly sliced
3 cloves garlic, crushed
1½ tablespoons Korean red pepper powder or 2 teaspoons cayenne
1 teaspoon grated fresh ginger root
1 teaspoon sugar
½ teaspoon salt

1. Mix all the ingredients together, and place in a pottery or glass container with a tight lid. Place in the refrigerator for 24 hours before serving.

Per half cup: Calories: 11, Protein: 0 g, Fat: 0 g, Carbohydrates: 2 g

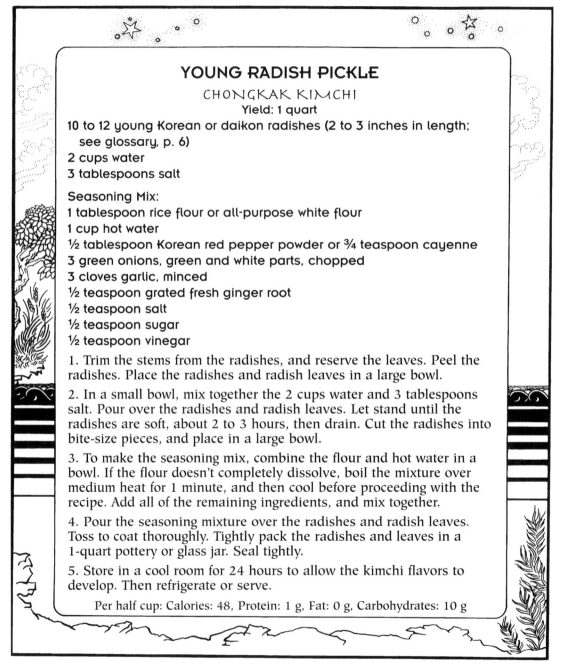

YOUNG RADISH PICKLE

CHONGKAK KIMCHI

Yield: 1 quart

10 to 12 young Korean or daikon radishes (2 to 3 inches in length;
   see glossary, p. 6)
2 cups water
3 tablespoons salt

Seasoning Mix:
1 tablespoon rice flour or all-purpose white flour
1 cup hot water
½ tablespoon Korean red pepper powder or ¾ teaspoon cayenne
3 green onions, green and white parts, chopped
3 cloves garlic, minced
½ teaspoon grated fresh ginger root
½ teaspoon salt
½ teaspoon sugar
½ teaspoon vinegar

1. Trim the stems from the radishes, and reserve the leaves. Peel the radishes. Place the radishes and radish leaves in a large bowl.

2. In a small bowl, mix together the 2 cups water and 3 tablespoons salt. Pour over the radishes and radish leaves. Let stand until the radishes are soft, about 2 to 3 hours, then drain. Cut the radishes into bite-size pieces, and place in a large bowl.

3. To make the seasoning mix, combine the flour and hot water in a bowl. If the flour doesn't completely dissolve, boil the mixture over medium heat for 1 minute, and then cool before proceeding with the recipe. Add all of the remaining ingredients, and mix together.

4. Pour the seasoning mixture over the radishes and radish leaves. Toss to coat thoroughly. Tightly pack the radishes and leaves in a 1-quart pottery or glass jar. Seal tightly.

5. Store in a cool room for 24 hours to allow the kimchi flavors to develop. Then refrigerate or serve.

Per half cup: Calories: 48, Protein: 1 g, Fat: 0 g, Carbohydrates: 10 g

EGGPLANT PICKLE

KAJI KIMCHI

Yield: 1 quart

2 medium Japanese eggplants
1 teaspoon salt

Stuffing:
¼ cup shredded Korean or daikon radish (see glossary, p. 6)
1 tablespoon chopped red bell pepper
2 green onions, green and white parts, chopped
2 cloves garlic, minced
½ teaspoon grated fresh ginger root
½ tablespoon Korean red pepper powder or ¾ teaspoon cayenne

1. Place the eggplants in a large saucepan, and add enough water to cover. Add the salt and bring to a boil. Cook for 2 to 3 minutes; the eggplants should still be firm. Drain and cool.

2. Cut each eggplant crosswise into 3 equal pieces (6 pieces total). Cut a deep criss-cross in the top of each piece without cutting all the way through. This will be where the stuffing will be placed, so it should be deep enough to accommodate the stuffing without the stuffing falling out the other side.

3. In a small bowl, mix the stuffing ingredients together. In each eggplant piece, firmly pack about 2 tablespoons of the stuffing into each crosscut.

4. Place the eggplant pieces in a 1-quart glass jar. Allow to ripen in a cool room for 24 hours. Then serve or refrigerate.

Per half cup: Calories: 40, Protein: 1 g, Fat: 0 g, Carbohydrates: 9 g

GREEN ONION PICKLE
PA KIMCHI

Yield: 1 quart

40 thin green onions
1 tablespoon salt
2 teaspoons Korean red pepper powder or 1 teaspoon cayenne
2 cloves garlic, crushed
1 teaspoon grated fresh ginger root
1 tablespoon sesame seeds
2 tablespoons water

1. Remove and discard the roots and any discolored stems from the green onions. Place the trimmed green onions in a bowl, sprinkle with salt, and let stand until the onions become limp, about 30 minutes. Rinse with cold water and drain. Place in a large bowl.

2. Add the Korean red pepper powder, garlic, and ginger. Mix well. Sprinkle the mixture with sesame seeds.

3. Bunch 5 onions together. Wrap the green stems around the onion bundle, leaving the white bulbs exposed. Repeat until there are 8 onion bundles.

4. Pack the onion bundles in a 1-quart jar. Add the water to the bowl that contained the onions, and swish the water around to collect any remaining spices. Pour the water over the onions. Seal the jar.

5. Place in a cool room for 3 days to allow to ripen. Refrigerate at least 24 hours before serving.

Per bundle: Calories: 19, Protein: 0 g, Fat: 0 g, Carbohydrates: 3 g

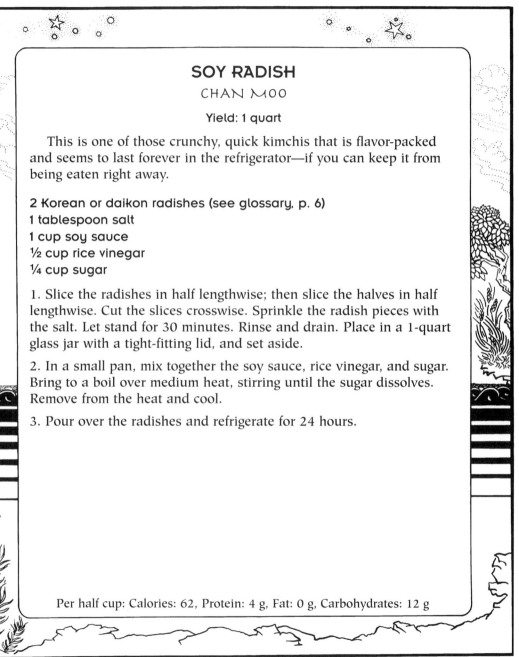

SOY RADISH

CHAN MOO

Yield: 1 quart

This is one of those crunchy, quick kimchis that is flavor-packed and seems to last forever in the refrigerator—if you can keep it from being eaten right away.

2 Korean or daikon radishes (see glossary, p. 6)
1 tablespoon salt
1 cup soy sauce
½ cup rice vinegar
¼ cup sugar

1. Slice the radishes in half lengthwise; then slice the halves in half lengthwise. Cut the slices crosswise. Sprinkle the radish pieces with the salt. Let stand for 30 minutes. Rinse and drain. Place in a 1-quart glass jar with a tight-fitting lid, and set aside.

2. In a small pan, mix together the soy sauce, rice vinegar, and sugar. Bring to a boil over medium heat, stirring until the sugar dissolves. Remove from the heat and cool.

3. Pour over the radishes and refrigerate for 24 hours.

Per half cup: Calories: 62, Protein: 4 g, Fat: 0 g, Carbohydrates: 12 g

STUFFED CABBAGE PICKLE

BOSAM KIMCHI

Yield: Approximately 2 quarts

This kimchi presents a kalidiscope of color and texture when ripened and ready to serve. Carefully slice the cabbage bundles so that the spiral pattern of cabbage leaves and stuffing is artfully exposed. Place in a bowl, drizzle with kimchi juice, and wait for the compliments.

2 Chinese cabbages (about 2½ to 3 pounds each)
4 cups water
¼ cup salt dissolved in ¼ cup water

Stuffing:
1 cucumber, shredded
1 Korean or daikon radish, shredded (see glossary, p. 6)
1 carrot, shredded
1 tablespoon sugar
1 tablespoon vinegar
½ tablespoon Korean red pepper powder or ¾ teaspoon cayenne
4 green onions, green and white parts, minced
2 cloves garlic, minced
½ teaspoon grated fresh ginger root
¼ cup red pepper threads, broken into pieces (optional; see red chili pepper, p. 7)
¼ cup water

1. Slice off the cabbage stems so the cabbage leaves are loose. Place the leaves in a large bowl. Pour the salt water over the cabbage leaves, making sure that the salt water gets between the cabbage leaves. Place a heavy plate on top if necessary to keep the cabbage under the brine. Let soak in a cool place, stirring occasionally, until

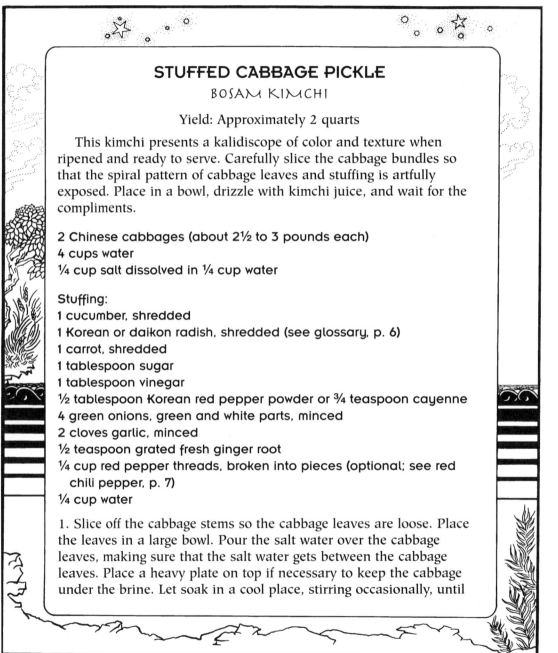

the cabbage is wilted and well-salted, about 6 hours. Drain and rinse the cabbage leaves in cool water; set aside.

2. To make the stuffing, mix together the cucumber, radish, carrot, sugar, vinegar, Korean red pepper powder, green onions, garlic, and ginger.

3. For each stuffed kimchi, use three cabbage leaves. Lay one cabbage leaf on a flat surface. Spread about 1 tablespoon of the stuffing mixture on the leaf. Lay another leaf on top of the first one, and spread on another tablespoon of stuffing. From the stem end, roll the cabbage into a bundle. Wrap the third leaf firmly around the bundle, and place in a large jar. Sprinkle a few chili threads on each stuffed kimchi. Repeat for each stuffed kimchi.

4. When all the stuffed kimchi are packed firmly in the jar, rinse the stuffing bowl with ¼ cup water. Pour this over the packed kimchi. Let stand in a cool room for 24 hours. More liquid will accumulate during this time. If the liquid does not cover the stuffed kimchi, make more brine by adding ½ teaspoon salt to 1 cup water; pour over the kimchi. Allow to ripen for 48 more hours, and then refrigerate before serving.

Per half cup: Calories: 18, Protein: 0 g, Fat: 0 g, Carbohydrates: 4 g

Vegetables, Salads & Side Dishes

YACHAE SANGCHAE E BANCHAN

One of the most appealing aspects of Korean dining is that there is such a broad assortment of side dishes from which to choose. The gracious Korean host or hostess will serve at least four or more side dishes as an appetizer course while the guest awaits the anticipated entrée. It seems that the measure of Korean hospitality is in direct proportion to the number and variety of side dishes presented and served at the table. This is not to say that the table is cluttered and carelessly laden with food. The vegetable side dishes are served in bowls measuring about three or four inches in diameter, conveniently and artfully arranged down the center of the table so that all guests can reach the tasty morsels with their chopsticks. At least one kimchi dish is served, along with three or four other vegetable side dishes, and maybe a hot or cold soup will be offered. Gratefully, the ubiquitous bowl of rice is always served to help quell the fire of some of the spicier side dishes. Sometimes lettuce or cabbage leaves are used as edible wrappers on which guests will spread denjang paste or gochujang. Rice and vegetables are layered on top, then the leaf and its contents are rolled into a cigar shape and eaten.

With such a colorful array of foods with appealing textures and tastes from which to choose, overindulgence can be a problem. Fortunately, these Korean vegetable dishes are healthfully low in fat and sugars and high in nutritious vitamins and minerals. So eat and enjoy—just save room for the main course.

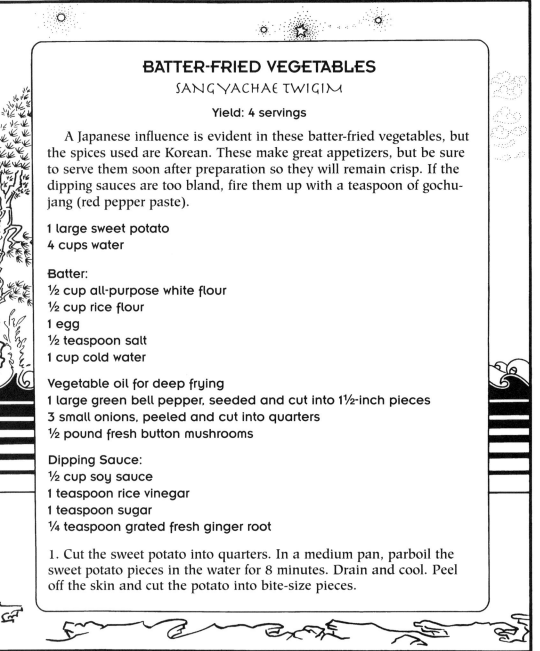

BATTER-FRIED VEGETABLES
SANG YACHAE TWIGIM
Yield: 4 servings

A Japanese influence is evident in these batter-fried vegetables, but the spices used are Korean. These make great appetizers, but be sure to serve them soon after preparation so they will remain crisp. If the dipping sauces are too bland, fire them up with a teaspoon of gochujang (red pepper paste).

1 large sweet potato
4 cups water

Batter:
½ cup all-purpose white flour
½ cup rice flour
1 egg
½ teaspoon salt
1 cup cold water

Vegetable oil for deep frying
1 large green bell pepper, seeded and cut into 1½-inch pieces
3 small onions, peeled and cut into quarters
½ pound fresh button mushrooms

Dipping Sauce:
½ cup soy sauce
1 teaspoon rice vinegar
1 teaspoon sugar
¼ teaspoon grated fresh ginger root

1. Cut the sweet potato into quarters. In a medium pan, parboil the sweet potato pieces in the water for 8 minutes. Drain and cool. Peel off the skin and cut the potato into bite-size pieces.

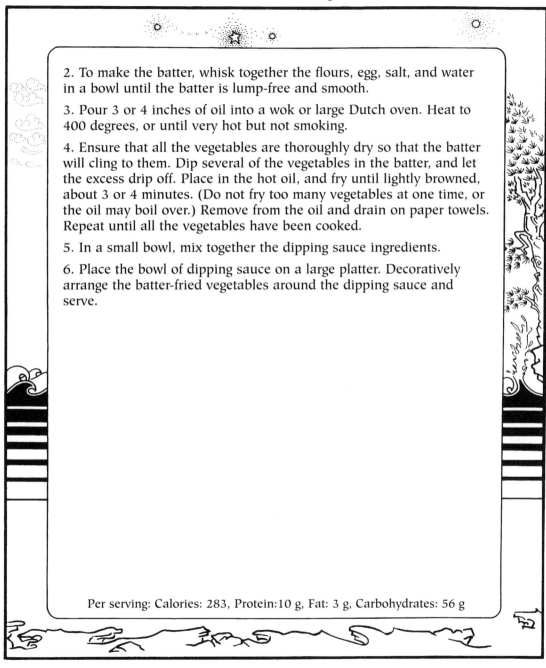

2. To make the batter, whisk together the flours, egg, salt, and water in a bowl until the batter is lump-free and smooth.

3. Pour 3 or 4 inches of oil into a wok or large Dutch oven. Heat to 400 degrees, or until very hot but not smoking.

4. Ensure that all the vegetables are thoroughly dry so that the batter will cling to them. Dip several of the vegetables in the batter, and let the excess drip off. Place in the hot oil, and fry until lightly browned, about 3 or 4 minutes. (Do not fry too many vegetables at one time, or the oil may boil over.) Remove from the oil and drain on paper towels. Repeat until all the vegetables have been cooked.

5. In a small bowl, mix together the dipping sauce ingredients.

6. Place the bowl of dipping sauce on a large platter. Decoratively arrange the batter-fried vegetables around the dipping sauce and serve.

Per serving: Calories: 283, Protein:10 g, Fat: 3 g, Carbohydrates: 56 g

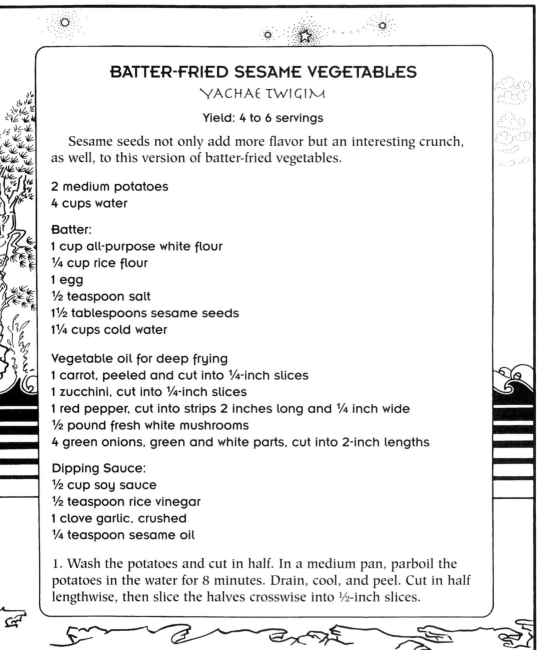

BATTER-FRIED SESAME VEGETABLES
YACHAE TWIGIM

Yield: 4 to 6 servings

Sesame seeds not only add more flavor but an interesting crunch, as well, to this version of batter-fried vegetables.

2 medium potatoes
4 cups water

Batter:
1 cup all-purpose white flour
¼ cup rice flour
1 egg
½ teaspoon salt
1½ tablespoons sesame seeds
1¼ cups cold water

Vegetable oil for deep frying
1 carrot, peeled and cut into ¼-inch slices
1 zucchini, cut into ¼-inch slices
1 red pepper, cut into strips 2 inches long and ¼ inch wide
½ pound fresh white mushrooms
4 green onions, green and white parts, cut into 2-inch lengths

Dipping Sauce:
½ cup soy sauce
½ teaspoon rice vinegar
1 clove garlic, crushed
¼ teaspoon sesame oil

1. Wash the potatoes and cut in half. In a medium pan, parboil the potatoes in the water for 8 minutes. Drain, cool, and peel. Cut in half lengthwise, then slice the halves crosswise into ½-inch slices.

2. Whisk together the batter ingredients until the batter is lump-free and smooth.

3. Pour 3 or 4 inches of oil into a wok or large Dutch oven, and heat to 400 degrees.

4. Ensure that all the vegetables are thoroughly dry so the batter will cling to them. Dip several of the vegetables in the batter, and let the excess drip off. Place in the hot oil, and fry until lightly browned, about 3 or 4 minutes. (Do not fry too many vegetables at one time or the oil may boil over.) Remove from the oil and drain on paper towels. Repeat until all vegetables have been cooked.

5. In a small bowl, mix together the dipping sauce ingredients.

6. Place the bowl of dipping sauce on a large platter. Decoratively arrange the batter-fried vegetables around the dipping sauce, and serve.

Per serving: Calories: 236, Protein: 9 g, Fat: 3 g, Carbohydrates: 42 g

BATTER-FRIED SPICY VEGETABLES
MAEUN YACHAE TWIGIM

Yield: 4 to 6 servings

Korean red pepper powder adds a bit of zing to the milder flavored vegetables used in this recipe. However, there is no reason any of the batters, vegetables, and sauces can't be mixed and matched. Be creative!

2 large potatoes
4 cups water

Batter:
½ cup all-purpose white flour
½ cup rice flour
1 egg
1 teaspoon garlic salt
½ teaspoon sugar
1 teaspoon Korean red pepper powder or ½ teaspoon cayenne
1 cup cold water

Vegetable oil for deep-frying
½ pound fresh button mushrooms
1 medium Japanese eggplant, cut into ¼-inch slices
1 medium white onion, cut in half and then quartered (a total of 8 bite-size pieces)
1 carrot, peeled and cut into ½-inch slices

Dipping Sauce:
½ cup soy sauce
1 teaspoon vinegar
½ teaspoon sugar
½ teaspoon sesame seeds

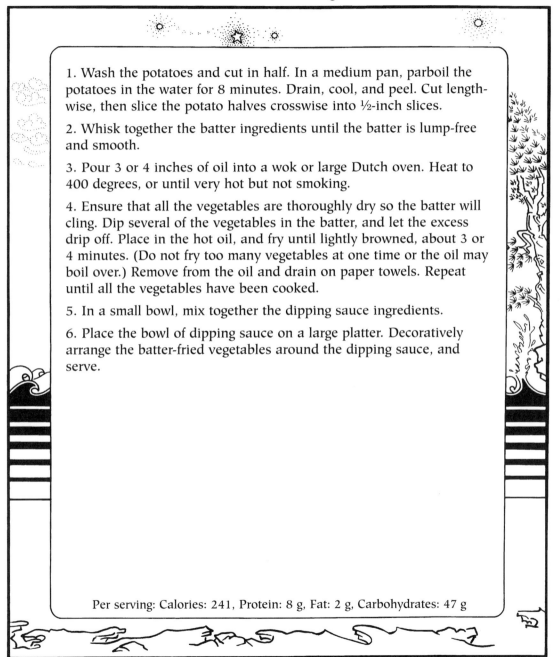

1. Wash the potatoes and cut in half. In a medium pan, parboil the potatoes in the water for 8 minutes. Drain, cool, and peel. Cut lengthwise, then slice the potato halves crosswise into ½-inch slices.

2. Whisk together the batter ingredients until the batter is lump-free and smooth.

3. Pour 3 or 4 inches of oil into a wok or large Dutch oven. Heat to 400 degrees, or until very hot but not smoking.

4. Ensure that all the vegetables are thoroughly dry so the batter will cling. Dip several of the vegetables in the batter, and let the excess drip off. Place in the hot oil, and fry until lightly browned, about 3 or 4 minutes. (Do not fry too many vegetables at one time or the oil may boil over.) Remove from the oil and drain on paper towels. Repeat until all the vegetables have been cooked.

5. In a small bowl, mix together the dipping sauce ingredients.

6. Place the bowl of dipping sauce on a large platter. Decoratively arrange the batter-fried vegetables around the dipping sauce, and serve.

Per serving: Calories: 241, Protein: 8 g, Fat: 2 g, Carbohydrates: 47 g

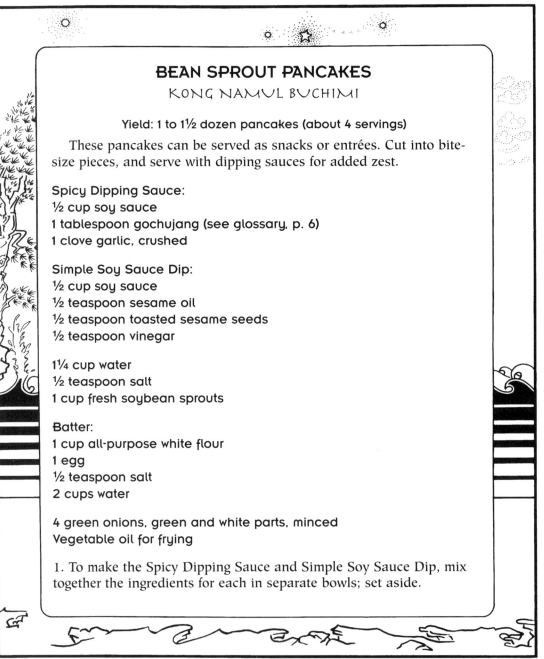

BEAN SPROUT PANCAKES
KONG NAMUL BUCHIMI

Yield: 1 to 1½ dozen pancakes (about 4 servings)

These pancakes can be served as snacks or entrées. Cut into bite-size pieces, and serve with dipping sauces for added zest.

Spicy Dipping Sauce:
½ cup soy sauce
1 tablespoon gochujang (see glossary, p. 6)
1 clove garlic, crushed

Simple Soy Sauce Dip:
½ cup soy sauce
½ teaspoon sesame oil
½ teaspoon toasted sesame seeds
½ teaspoon vinegar

1¼ cup water
½ teaspoon salt
1 cup fresh soybean sprouts

Batter:
1 cup all-purpose white flour
1 egg
½ teaspoon salt
2 cups water

4 green onions, green and white parts, minced
Vegetable oil for frying

1. To make the Spicy Dipping Sauce and Simple Soy Sauce Dip, mix together the ingredients for each in separate bowls; set aside.

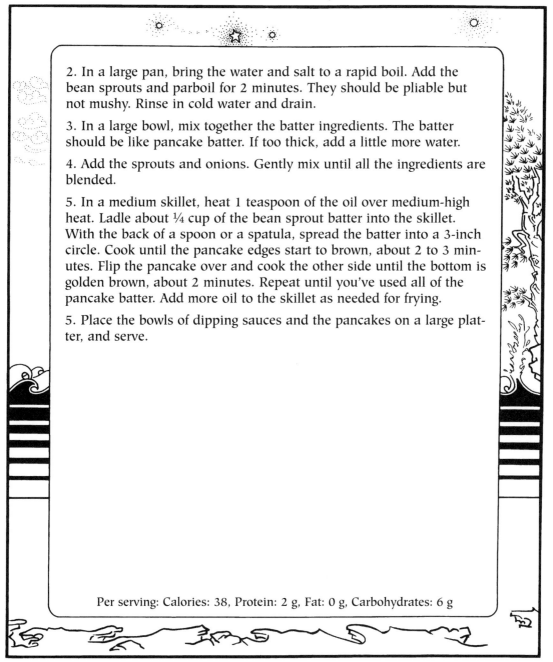

2. In a large pan, bring the water and salt to a rapid boil. Add the bean sprouts and parboil for 2 minutes. They should be pliable but not mushy. Rinse in cold water and drain.

3. In a large bowl, mix together the batter ingredients. The batter should be like pancake batter. If too thick, add a little more water.

4. Add the sprouts and onions. Gently mix until all the ingredients are blended.

5. In a medium skillet, heat 1 teaspoon of the oil over medium-high heat. Ladle about ¼ cup of the bean sprout batter into the skillet. With the back of a spoon or a spatula, spread the batter into a 3-inch circle. Cook until the pancake edges start to brown, about 2 to 3 minutes. Flip the pancake over and cook the other side until the bottom is golden brown, about 2 minutes. Repeat until you've used all of the pancake batter. Add more oil to the skillet as needed for frying.

5. Place the bowls of dipping sauces and the pancakes on a large platter, and serve.

Per serving: Calories: 38, Protein: 2 g, Fat: 0 g, Carbohydrates: 6 g

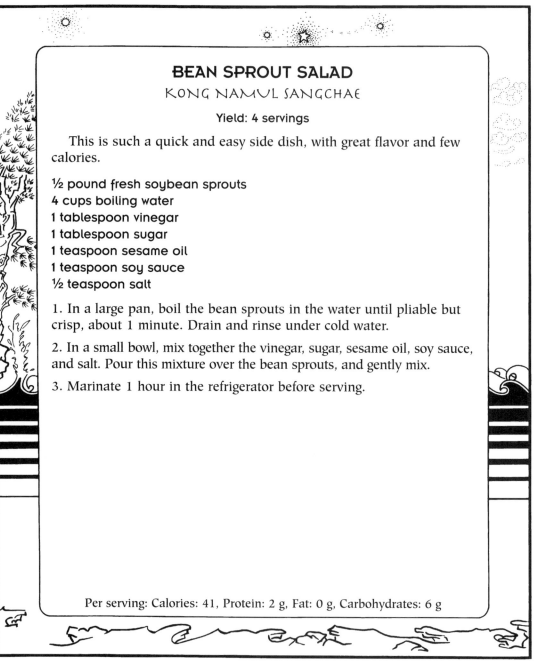

BEAN SPROUT SALAD
KONG NAMUL SANGCHAE

Yield: 4 servings

This is such a quick and easy side dish, with great flavor and few calories.

½ pound fresh soybean sprouts
4 cups boiling water
1 tablespoon vinegar
1 tablespoon sugar
1 teaspoon sesame oil
1 teaspoon soy sauce
½ teaspoon salt

1. In a large pan, boil the bean sprouts in the water until pliable but crisp, about 1 minute. Drain and rinse under cold water.

2. In a small bowl, mix together the vinegar, sugar, sesame oil, soy sauce, and salt. Pour this mixture over the bean sprouts, and gently mix.

3. Marinate 1 hour in the refrigerator before serving.

Per serving: Calories: 41, Protein: 2 g, Fat: 0 g, Carbohydrates: 6 g

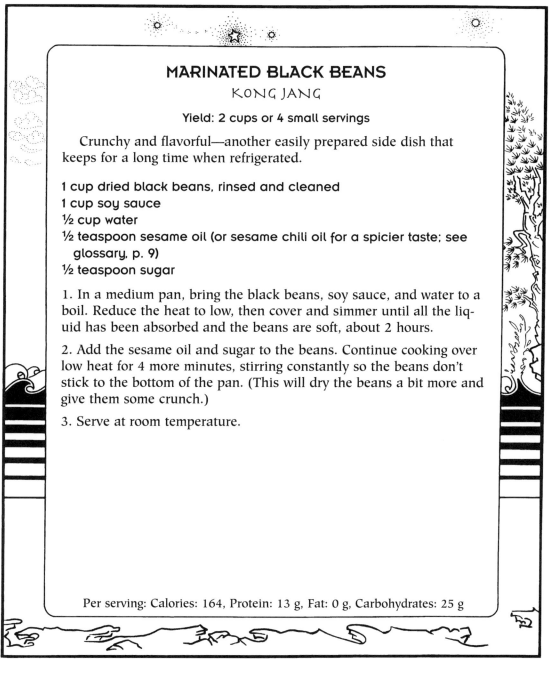

MARINATED BLACK BEANS

KONG JANG

Yield: 2 cups or 4 small servings

Crunchy and flavorful—another easily prepared side dish that keeps for a long time when refrigerated.

1 cup dried black beans, rinsed and cleaned
1 cup soy sauce
½ cup water
½ teaspoon sesame oil (or sesame chili oil for a spicier taste; see glossary, p. 9)
½ teaspoon sugar

1. In a medium pan, bring the black beans, soy sauce, and water to a boil. Reduce the heat to low, then cover and simmer until all the liquid has been absorbed and the beans are soft, about 2 hours.

2. Add the sesame oil and sugar to the beans. Continue cooking over low heat for 4 more minutes, stirring constantly so the beans don't stick to the bottom of the pan. (This will dry the beans a bit more and give them some crunch.)

3. Serve at room temperature.

Per serving: Calories: 164, Protein: 13 g, Fat: 0 g, Carbohydrates: 25 g

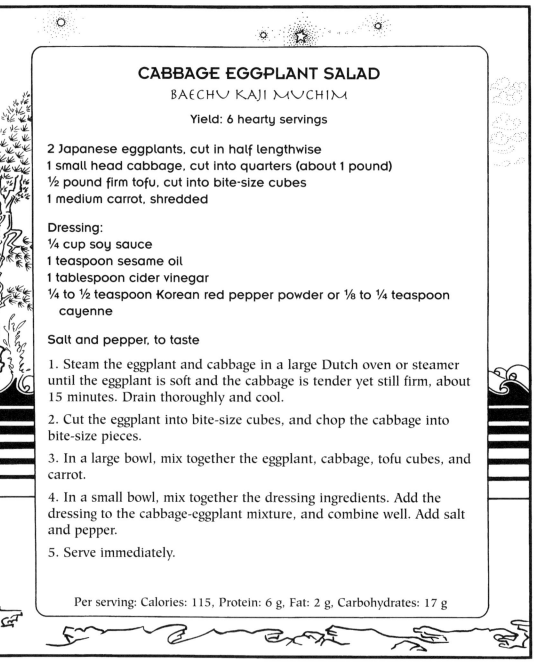

CABBAGE EGGPLANT SALAD

BAECHU KAJI MUCHIM

Yield: 6 hearty servings

2 Japanese eggplants, cut in half lengthwise
1 small head cabbage, cut into quarters (about 1 pound)
½ pound firm tofu, cut into bite-size cubes
1 medium carrot, shredded

Dressing:
¼ cup soy sauce
1 teaspoon sesame oil
1 tablespoon cider vinegar
¼ to ½ teaspoon Korean red pepper powder or ⅛ to ¼ teaspoon
   cayenne

Salt and pepper, to taste

1. Steam the eggplant and cabbage in a large Dutch oven or steamer until the eggplant is soft and the cabbage is tender yet still firm, about 15 minutes. Drain thoroughly and cool.

2. Cut the eggplant into bite-size cubes, and chop the cabbage into bite-size pieces.

3. In a large bowl, mix together the eggplant, cabbage, tofu cubes, and carrot.

4. In a small bowl, mix together the dressing ingredients. Add the dressing to the cabbage-eggplant mixture, and combine well. Add salt and pepper.

5. Serve immediately.

Per serving: Calories: 115, Protein: 6 g, Fat: 2 g, Carbohydrates: 17 g

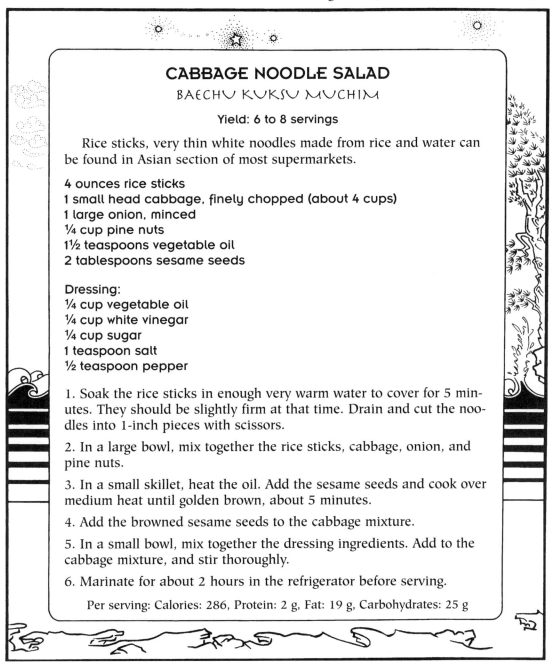

CABBAGE NOODLE SALAD

BAECHU KUKSU MUCHIM

Yield: 6 to 8 servings

Rice sticks, very thin white noodles made from rice and water can be found in Asian section of most supermarkets.

4 ounces rice sticks
1 small head cabbage, finely chopped (about 4 cups)
1 large onion, minced
¼ cup pine nuts
1½ teaspoons vegetable oil
2 tablespoons sesame seeds

Dressing:
¼ cup vegetable oil
¼ cup white vinegar
¼ cup sugar
1 teaspoon salt
½ teaspoon pepper

1. Soak the rice sticks in enough very warm water to cover for 5 minutes. They should be slightly firm at that time. Drain and cut the noodles into 1-inch pieces with scissors.

2. In a large bowl, mix together the rice sticks, cabbage, onion, and pine nuts.

3. In a small skillet, heat the oil. Add the sesame seeds and cook over medium heat until golden brown, about 5 minutes.

4. Add the browned sesame seeds to the cabbage mixture.

5. In a small bowl, mix together the dressing ingredients. Add to the cabbage mixture, and stir thoroughly.

6. Marinate for about 2 hours in the refrigerator before serving.

Per serving: Calories: 286, Protein: 2 g, Fat: 19 g, Carbohydrates: 25 g

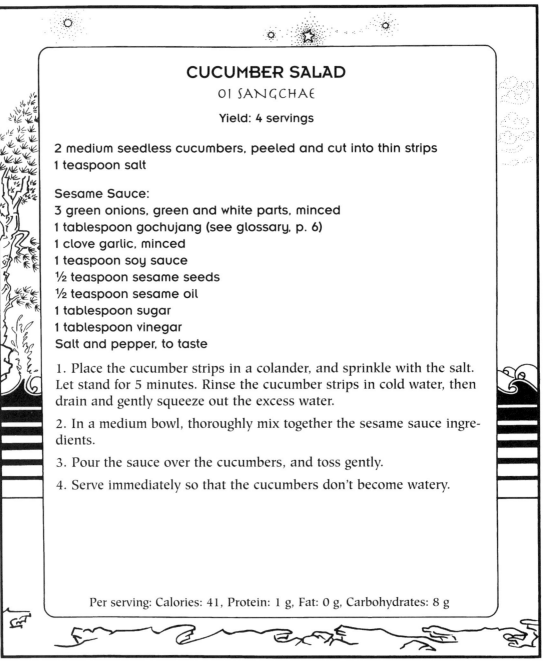

CUCUMBER SALAD
OI SANGCHAE

Yield: 4 servings

2 medium seedless cucumbers, peeled and cut into thin strips
1 teaspoon salt

Sesame Sauce:
3 green onions, green and white parts, minced
1 tablespoon gochujang (see glossary, p. 6)
1 clove garlic, minced
1 teaspoon soy sauce
½ teaspoon sesame seeds
½ teaspoon sesame oil
1 tablespoon sugar
1 tablespoon vinegar
Salt and pepper, to taste

1. Place the cucumber strips in a colander, and sprinkle with the salt. Let stand for 5 minutes. Rinse the cucumber strips in cold water, then drain and gently squeeze out the excess water.

2. In a medium bowl, thoroughly mix together the sesame sauce ingredients.

3. Pour the sauce over the cucumbers, and toss gently.

4. Serve immediately so that the cucumbers don't become watery.

Per serving: Calories: 41, Protein: 1 g, Fat: 0 g, Carbohydrates: 8 g

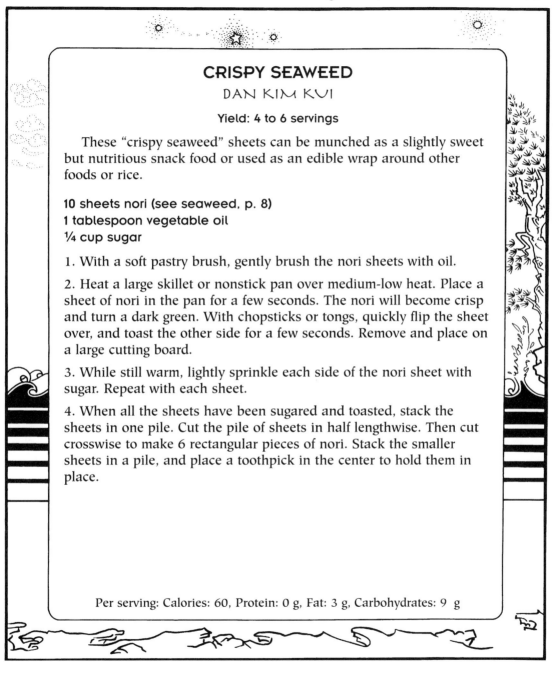

CRISPY SEAWEED

DAN KIM KUI

Yield: 4 to 6 servings

These "crispy seaweed" sheets can be munched as a slightly sweet but nutritious snack food or used as an edible wrap around other foods or rice.

10 sheets nori (see seaweed, p. 8)
1 tablespoon vegetable oil
¼ cup sugar

1. With a soft pastry brush, gently brush the nori sheets with oil.

2. Heat a large skillet or nonstick pan over medium-low heat. Place a sheet of nori in the pan for a few seconds. The nori will become crisp and turn a dark green. With chopsticks or tongs, quickly flip the sheet over, and toast the other side for a few seconds. Remove and place on a large cutting board.

3. While still warm, lightly sprinkle each side of the nori sheet with sugar. Repeat with each sheet.

4. When all the sheets have been sugared and toasted, stack the sheets in one pile. Cut the pile of sheets in half lengthwise. Then cut crosswise to make 6 rectangular pieces of nori. Stack the smaller sheets in a pile, and place a toothpick in the center to hold them in place.

Per serving: Calories: 60, Protein: 0 g, Fat: 3 g, Carbohydrates: 9 g

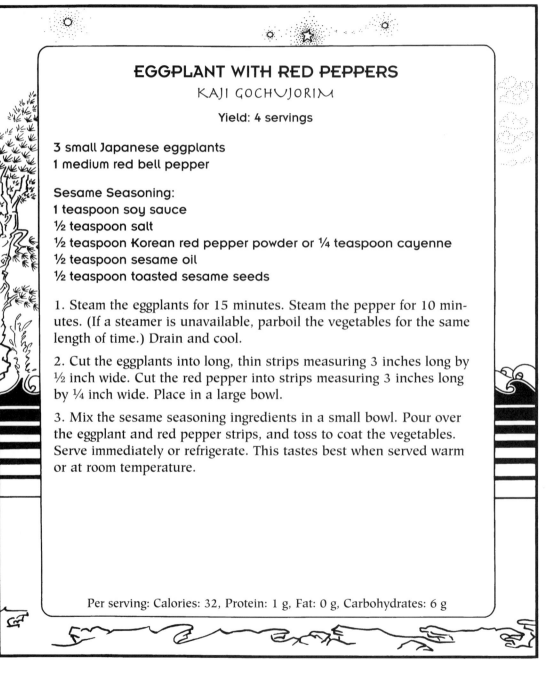

EGGPLANT WITH RED PEPPERS

KAJI GOCHUJORIM

Yield: 4 servings

3 small Japanese eggplants
1 medium red bell pepper

Sesame Seasoning:
1 teaspoon soy sauce
½ teaspoon salt
½ teaspoon Korean red pepper powder or ¼ teaspoon cayenne
½ teaspoon sesame oil
½ teaspoon toasted sesame seeds

1. Steam the eggplants for 15 minutes. Steam the pepper for 10 minutes. (If a steamer is unavailable, parboil the vegetables for the same length of time.) Drain and cool.

2. Cut the eggplants into long, thin strips measuring 3 inches long by ½ inch wide. Cut the red pepper into strips measuring 3 inches long by ¼ inch wide. Place in a large bowl.

3. Mix the sesame seasoning ingredients in a small bowl. Pour over the eggplant and red pepper strips, and toss to coat the vegetables. Serve immediately or refrigerate. This tastes best when served warm or at room temperature.

Per serving: Calories: 32, Protein: 1 g, Fat: 0 g, Carbohydrates: 6 g

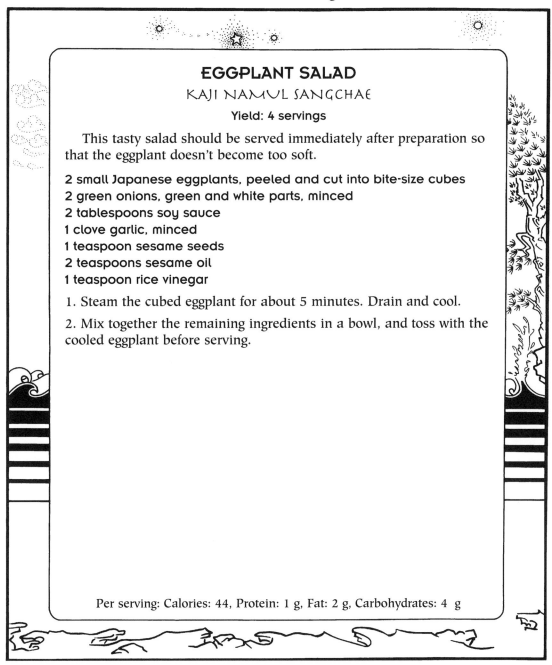

EGGPLANT SALAD

KAJI NAMUL SANGCHAE

Yield: 4 servings

This tasty salad should be served immediately after preparation so that the eggplant doesn't become too soft.

2 small Japanese eggplants, peeled and cut into bite-size cubes
2 green onions, green and white parts, minced
2 tablespoons soy sauce
1 clove garlic, minced
1 teaspoon sesame seeds
2 teaspoons sesame oil
1 teaspoon rice vinegar

1. Steam the cubed eggplant for about 5 minutes. Drain and cool.

2. Mix together the remaining ingredients in a bowl, and toss with the cooled eggplant before serving.

Per serving: Calories: 44, Protein: 1 g, Fat: 2 g, Carbohydrates: 4 g

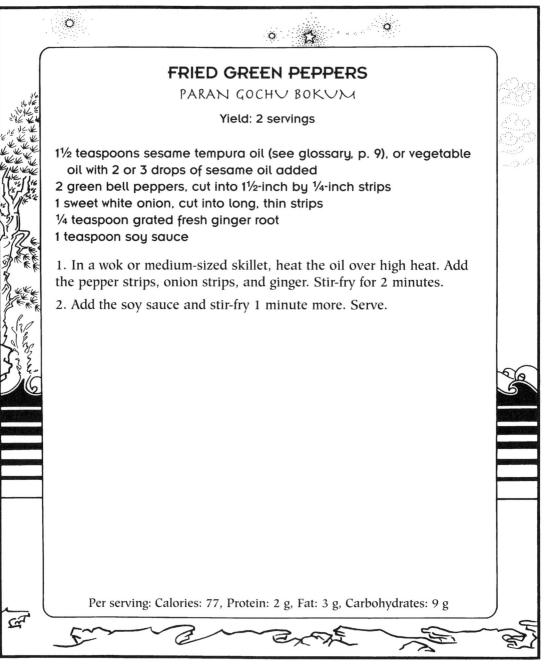

FRIED GREEN PEPPERS

PARAN GOCHU BOKUM

Yield: 2 servings

1½ teaspoons sesame tempura oil (see glossary, p. 9), or vegetable
    oil with 2 or 3 drops of sesame oil added
2 green bell peppers, cut into 1½-inch by ¼-inch strips
1 sweet white onion, cut into long, thin strips
¼ teaspoon grated fresh ginger root
1 teaspoon soy sauce

1. In a wok or medium-sized skillet, heat the oil over high heat. Add the pepper strips, onion strips, and ginger. Stir-fry for 2 minutes.

2. Add the soy sauce and stir-fry 1 minute more. Serve.

Per serving: Calories: 77, Protein: 2 g, Fat: 3 g, Carbohydrates: 9 g

FRIED RED PEPPER POTATOES

KAMJA BOKUM

Yield: 4 servings

1½ tablespoons vegetable oil
3 large or 4 medium potatoes, peeled and cut into bite-size cubes
1 large red bell pepper, chopped
4 green onions, green and white parts, chopped
2 teaspoons sesame seeds
1½ tablespoons soy sauce
1 teaspoon Korean red pepper powder or ½ teaspoon cayenne
½ teaspoon salt

1. In a wok or large skillet, heat the oil over medium-high heat. Add the potatoes and bell pepper. Stir-fry until the potatoes are a light golden brown, about 4 minutes.

2. Add the onions and sesame seeds, and cook 1 minute more.

3. In a cup or small bowl, mix together the soy sauce, Korean red pepper powder, and salt. Add to the potato mixture, and stir. Cook until all the liquid has been absorbed, about 1 or 2 minutes. Serve warm.

Per serving: Calories: 181, Protein: 2 g, Fat: 5 g, Carbohydrates: 29 g

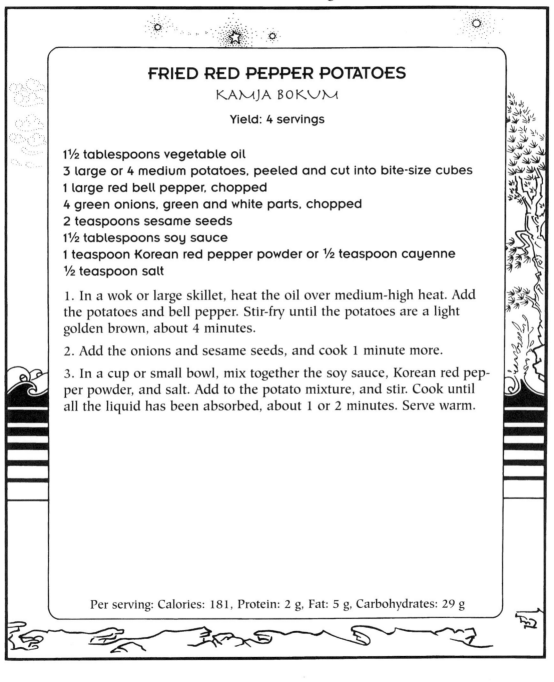

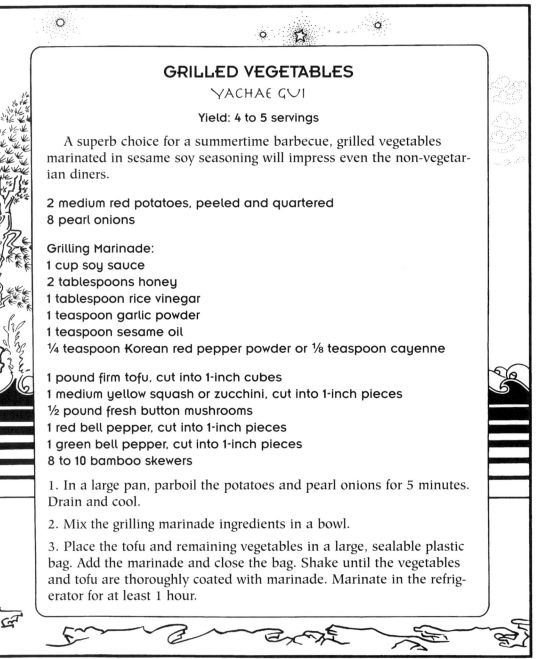

GRILLED VEGETABLES

YACHAE GUI

Yield: 4 to 5 servings

A superb choice for a summertime barbecue, grilled vegetables marinated in sesame soy seasoning will impress even the non-vegetarian diners.

2 medium red potatoes, peeled and quartered
8 pearl onions

Grilling Marinade:
1 cup soy sauce
2 tablespoons honey
1 tablespoon rice vinegar
1 teaspoon garlic powder
1 teaspoon sesame oil
¼ teaspoon Korean red pepper powder or ⅛ teaspoon cayenne

1 pound firm tofu, cut into 1-inch cubes
1 medium yellow squash or zucchini, cut into 1-inch pieces
½ pound fresh button mushrooms
1 red bell pepper, cut into 1-inch pieces
1 green bell pepper, cut into 1-inch pieces
8 to 10 bamboo skewers

1. In a large pan, parboil the potatoes and pearl onions for 5 minutes. Drain and cool.

2. Mix the grilling marinade ingredients in a bowl.

3. Place the tofu and remaining vegetables in a large, sealable plastic bag. Add the marinade and close the bag. Shake until the vegetables and tofu are thoroughly coated with marinade. Marinate in the refrigerator for at least 1 hour.

4. Soak the bamboo skewers for at least 15 minutes in cold water. This will help keep them from burning while on the grill.

5. Alternately thread the vegetables and tofu cubes onto the skewers.

6. Grill the vegetables on a barbecue grill or under a broiler, turning to brown evenly, then serve.

Per serving: Calories: 243, Protein: 15 g, Fat: 5 g, Carbohydrates: 32 g

MUNG BEAN CURD
MUK MUCHIM

Yield: 2 main-dish servings or 4 side-dish servings

Mung bean curd is made from mung bean starch and sold in rectangular blocks at most Asian markets. If fresh mung bean curd is not available, packages of mung bean starch with English instructions can be purchased, and the bean curd can be made fresh in your kitchen. Like tofu, mung bean curd readily absorbs seasonings and can be used for some flavor-packed recipes such as this one.

½ pound mung bean curd, sliced into 1-inch squares, ¼-inch thick
(see glossary, p. 7)

Seasoned Sauce:
3 tablespoons soy sauce
1 teaspoon sesame oil
½ teaspoon sugar
4 green onions, green and white parts, minced
1 clove garlic, minced
1 teaspoon toasted sesame seeds
½ to 1 teaspoon Korean red pepper powder or ¼ to ½ teaspoon
  cayenne

1. Place the mung bean curd squares in a shallow bowl.

2. Mix the seasoned sauce ingredients together in a small bowl.

3. Pour the seasoned sauce over the mung bean curd, and serve.

Per 3 servings: Calories: 132, Protein: 7 g, Fat: 8 g, Carbohydrates: 5 g

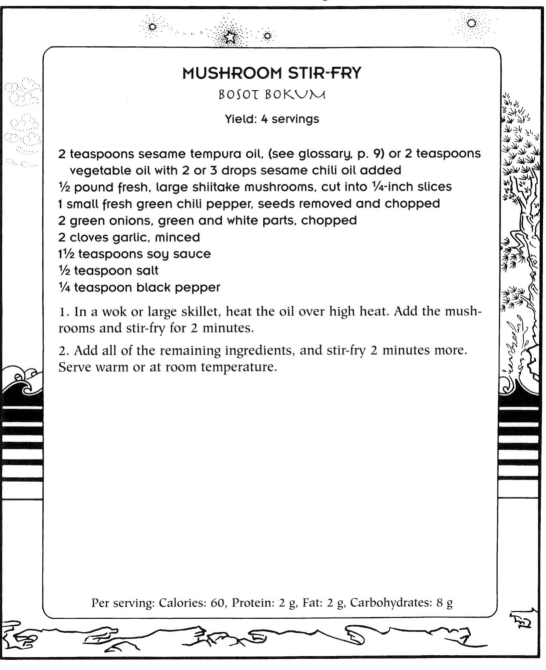

MUSHROOM STIR-FRY

BOSOT BOKUM

Yield: 4 servings

2 teaspoons sesame tempura oil, (see glossary, p. 9) or 2 teaspoons
 vegetable oil with 2 or 3 drops sesame chili oil added
½ pound fresh, large shiitake mushrooms, cut into ¼-inch slices
1 small fresh green chili pepper, seeds removed and chopped
2 green onions, green and white parts, chopped
2 cloves garlic, minced
1½ teaspoons soy sauce
½ teaspoon salt
¼ teaspoon black pepper

1. In a wok or large skillet, heat the oil over high heat. Add the mushrooms and stir-fry for 2 minutes.

2. Add all of the remaining ingredients, and stir-fry 2 minutes more. Serve warm or at room temperature.

Per serving: Calories: 60, Protein: 2 g, Fat: 2 g, Carbohydrates: 8 g

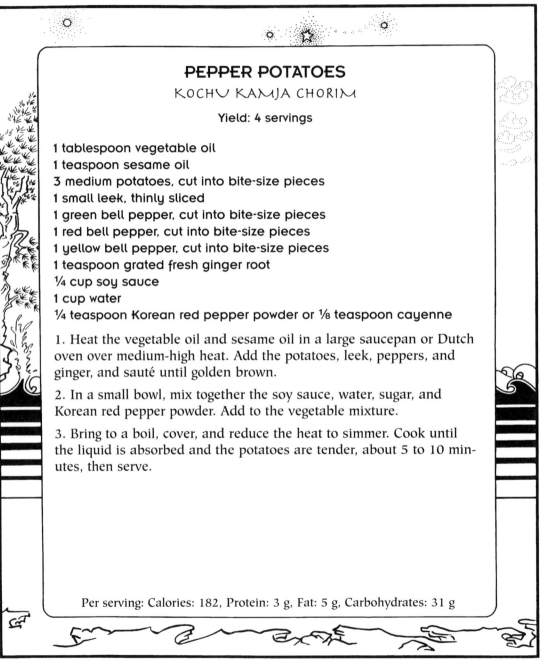

PEPPER POTATOES
KOCHU KAMJA CHORIM

Yield: 4 servings

1 tablespoon vegetable oil
1 teaspoon sesame oil
3 medium potatoes, cut into bite-size pieces
1 small leek, thinly sliced
1 green bell pepper, cut into bite-size pieces
1 red bell pepper, cut into bite-size pieces
1 yellow bell pepper, cut into bite-size pieces
1 teaspoon grated fresh ginger root
¼ cup soy sauce
1 cup water
¼ teaspoon Korean red pepper powder or ⅛ teaspoon cayenne

1. Heat the vegetable oil and sesame oil in a large saucepan or Dutch oven over medium-high heat. Add the potatoes, leek, peppers, and ginger, and sauté until golden brown.

2. In a small bowl, mix together the soy sauce, water, sugar, and Korean red pepper powder. Add to the vegetable mixture.

3. Bring to a boil, cover, and reduce the heat to simmer. Cook until the liquid is absorbed and the potatoes are tender, about 5 to 10 minutes, then serve.

Per serving: Calories: 182, Protein: 3 g, Fat: 5 g, Carbohydrates: 31 g

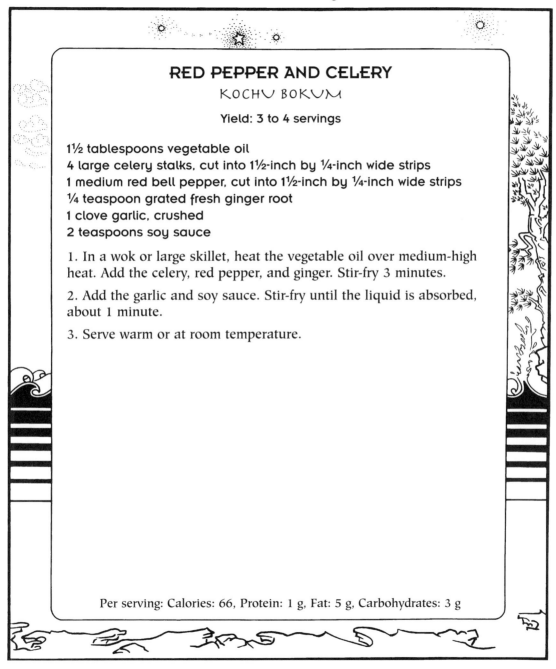

RED PEPPER AND CELERY

KOCHU BOKUM

Yield: 3 to 4 servings

1½ tablespoons vegetable oil
4 large celery stalks, cut into 1½-inch by ¼-inch wide strips
1 medium red bell pepper, cut into 1½-inch by ¼-inch wide strips
¼ teaspoon grated fresh ginger root
1 clove garlic, crushed
2 teaspoons soy sauce

1. In a wok or large skillet, heat the vegetable oil over medium-high heat. Add the celery, red pepper, and ginger. Stir-fry 3 minutes.

2. Add the garlic and soy sauce. Stir-fry until the liquid is absorbed, about 1 minute.

3. Serve warm or at room temperature.

Per serving: Calories: 66, Protein: 1 g, Fat: 5 g, Carbohydrates: 3 g

RED PEPPER BROCCOLI

YACHAE KOCHU BOKUM

Yield: 4 servings

1½ tablespoons vegetable oil

1 large red bell pepper, cut into 1½-inch by ¼-inch wide strips
4 cups broccoli flowerets, cut into bite-size pieces
1 small white onion, cut in half lengthwise and then thinly sliced
   crosswise
½ teaspoon grated fresh ginger root
2 cloves garlic, minced
½ teaspoon Korean red pepper powder or ¼ teaspoon cayenne
1 tablespoon soy sauce
1 tablespoon pine nuts (see glossary, p. 7)

1. In a wok or large skillet, heat the oil over medium-high heat. Add the red pepper and broccoli. Stir-fry until the vegetables are crisp-tender, about 5 minutes.

2. Add the onion and ginger. Stir-fry 2 minutes more.

3. In a small bowl, mix together the garlic, Korean red pepper powder, and soy sauce. Add to the vegetables. Cook until the liquid is absorbed, about 1 minute.

4. Sprinkle with the pine nuts, and serve.

Per serving: Calories: 103, Protein: 3 g, Fat: 6 g, Carbohydrates: 8 g

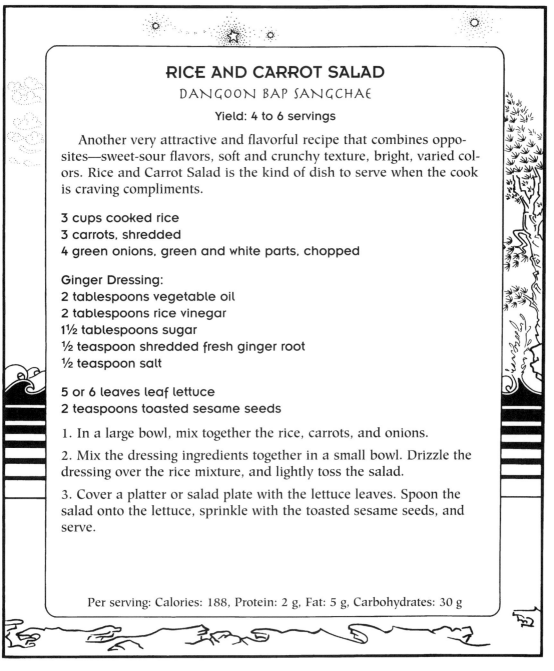

RICE AND CARROT SALAD

DANGOON BAP SANGCHAE

Yield: 4 to 6 servings

Another very attractive and flavorful recipe that combines opposites—sweet-sour flavors, soft and crunchy texture, bright, varied colors. Rice and Carrot Salad is the kind of dish to serve when the cook is craving compliments.

3 cups cooked rice
3 carrots, shredded
4 green onions, green and white parts, chopped

Ginger Dressing:
2 tablespoons vegetable oil
2 tablespoons rice vinegar
1½ tablespoons sugar
½ teaspoon shredded fresh ginger root
½ teaspoon salt

5 or 6 leaves leaf lettuce
2 teaspoons toasted sesame seeds

1. In a large bowl, mix together the rice, carrots, and onions.

2. Mix the dressing ingredients together in a small bowl. Drizzle the dressing over the rice mixture, and lightly toss the salad.

3. Cover a platter or salad plate with the lettuce leaves. Spoon the salad onto the lettuce, sprinkle with the toasted sesame seeds, and serve.

Per serving: Calories: 188, Protein: 2 g, Fat: 5 g, Carbohydrates: 30 g

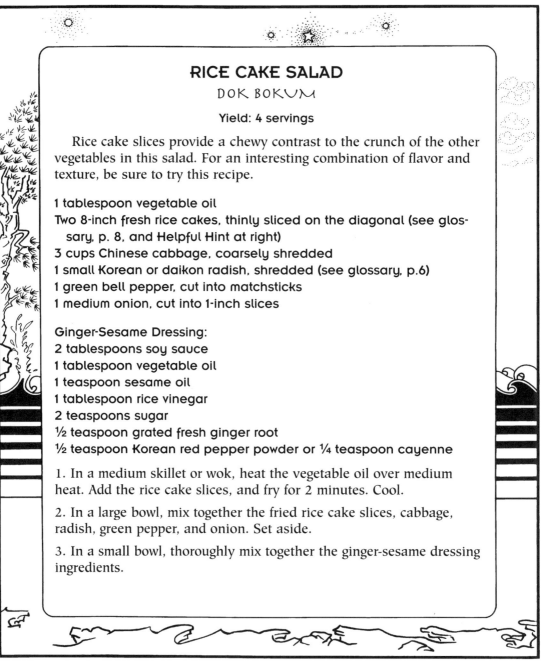

RICE CAKE SALAD
DOK BOKUM

Yield: 4 servings

Rice cake slices provide a chewy contrast to the crunch of the other vegetables in this salad. For an interesting combination of flavor and texture, be sure to try this recipe.

1 tablespoon vegetable oil
Two 8-inch fresh rice cakes, thinly sliced on the diagonal (see glossary, p. 8, and Helpful Hint at right)
3 cups Chinese cabbage, coarsely shredded
1 small Korean or daikon radish, shredded (see glossary, p.6)
1 green bell pepper, cut into matchsticks
1 medium onion, cut into 1-inch slices

Ginger-Sesame Dressing:
2 tablespoons soy sauce
1 tablespoon vegetable oil
1 teaspoon sesame oil
1 tablespoon rice vinegar
2 teaspoons sugar
½ teaspoon grated fresh ginger root
½ teaspoon Korean red pepper powder or ¼ teaspoon cayenne

1. In a medium skillet or wok, heat the vegetable oil over medium heat. Add the rice cake slices, and fry for 2 minutes. Cool.

2. In a large bowl, mix together the fried rice cake slices, cabbage, radish, green pepper, and onion. Set aside.

3. In a small bowl, thoroughly mix together the ginger-sesame dressing ingredients.

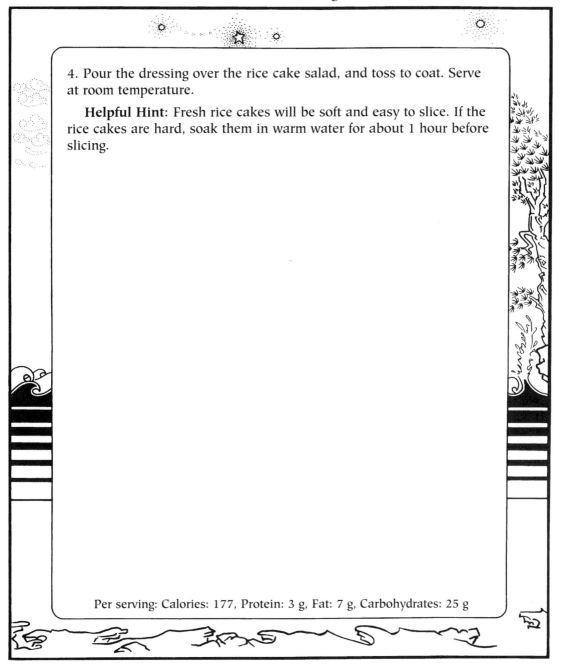

4. Pour the dressing over the rice cake salad, and toss to coat. Serve at room temperature.

Helpful Hint: Fresh rice cakes will be soft and easy to slice. If the rice cakes are hard, soak them in warm water for about 1 hour before slicing.

Per serving: Calories: 177, Protein: 3 g, Fat: 7 g, Carbohydrates: 25 g

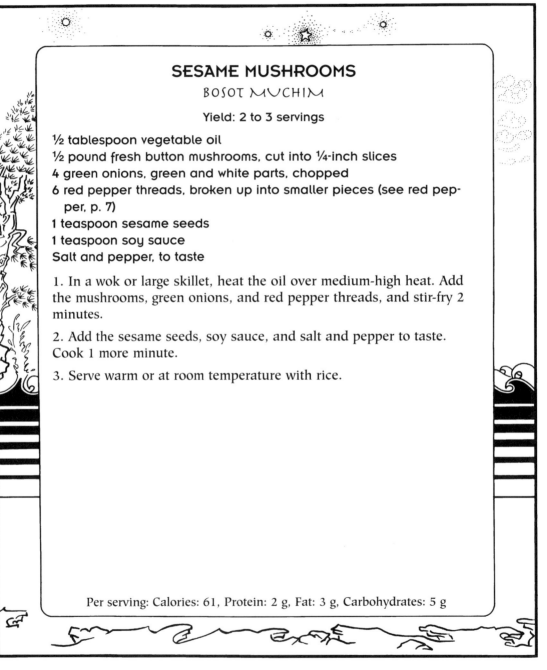

SESAME MUSHROOMS

BOSOT MUCHIM

Yield: 2 to 3 servings

½ tablespoon vegetable oil
½ pound fresh button mushrooms, cut into ¼-inch slices
4 green onions, green and white parts, chopped
6 red pepper threads, broken up into smaller pieces (see red pepper, p. 7)
1 teaspoon sesame seeds
1 teaspoon soy sauce
Salt and pepper, to taste

1. In a wok or large skillet, heat the oil over medium-high heat. Add the mushrooms, green onions, and red pepper threads, and stir-fry 2 minutes.

2. Add the sesame seeds, soy sauce, and salt and pepper to taste. Cook 1 more minute.

3. Serve warm or at room temperature with rice.

Per serving: Calories: 61, Protein: 2 g, Fat: 3 g, Carbohydrates: 5 g

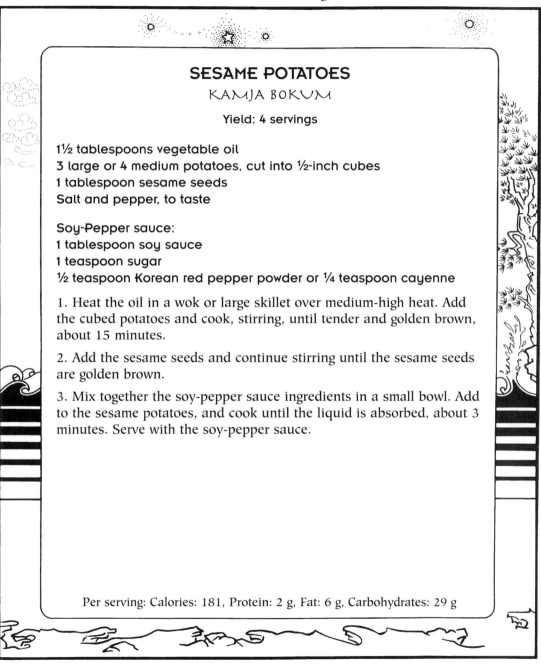

SESAME POTATOES

KAMJA BOKUM

Yield: 4 servings

1½ tablespoons vegetable oil
3 large or 4 medium potatoes, cut into ½-inch cubes
1 tablespoon sesame seeds
Salt and pepper, to taste

Soy-Pepper sauce:
1 tablespoon soy sauce
1 teaspoon sugar
½ teaspoon Korean red pepper powder or ¼ teaspoon cayenne

1. Heat the oil in a wok or large skillet over medium-high heat. Add the cubed potatoes and cook, stirring, until tender and golden brown, about 15 minutes.

2. Add the sesame seeds and continue stirring until the sesame seeds are golden brown.

3. Mix together the soy-pepper sauce ingredients in a small bowl. Add to the sesame potatoes, and cook until the liquid is absorbed, about 3 minutes. Serve with the soy-pepper sauce.

Per serving: Calories: 181, Protein: 2 g, Fat: 6 g, Carbohydrates: 29 g

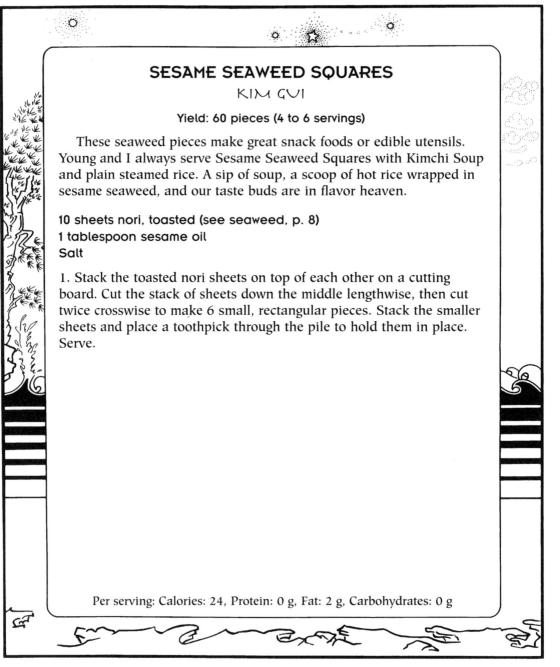

SESAME SEAWEED SQUARES
KIM GUI

Yield: 60 pieces (4 to 6 servings)

These seaweed pieces make great snack foods or edible utensils. Young and I always serve Sesame Seaweed Squares with Kimchi Soup and plain steamed rice. A sip of soup, a scoop of hot rice wrapped in sesame seaweed, and our taste buds are in flavor heaven.

10 sheets nori, toasted (see seaweed, p. 8)
1 tablespoon sesame oil
Salt

1. Stack the toasted nori sheets on top of each other on a cutting board. Cut the stack of sheets down the middle lengthwise, then cut twice crosswise to make 6 small, rectangular pieces. Stack the smaller sheets and place a toothpick through the pile to hold them in place. Serve.

Per serving: Calories: 24, Protein: 0 g, Fat: 2 g, Carbohydrates: 0 g

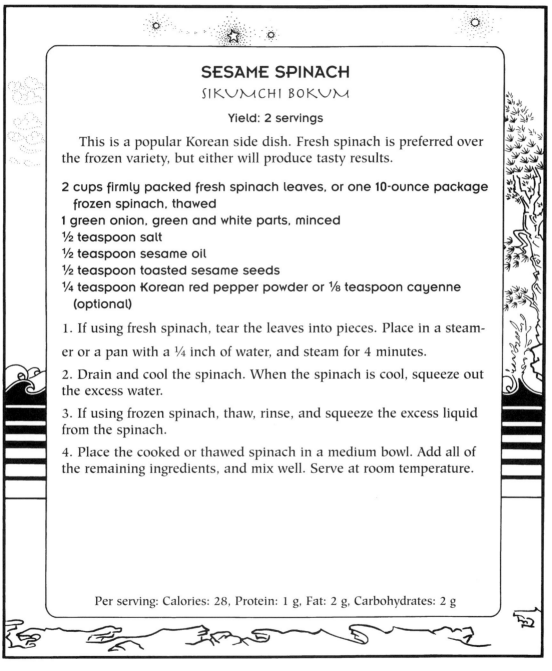

SESAME SPINACH

SIKUMCHI BOKUM

Yield: 2 servings

This is a popular Korean side dish. Fresh spinach is preferred over the frozen variety, but either will produce tasty results.

2 cups firmly packed fresh spinach leaves, or one 10-ounce package
    frozen spinach, thawed
1 green onion, green and white parts, minced
½ teaspoon salt
½ teaspoon sesame oil
½ teaspoon toasted sesame seeds
¼ teaspoon Korean red pepper powder or ⅛ teaspoon cayenne
    (optional)

1. If using fresh spinach, tear the leaves into pieces. Place in a steamer or a pan with a ¼ inch of water, and steam for 4 minutes.

2. Drain and cool the spinach. When the spinach is cool, squeeze out the excess water.

3. If using frozen spinach, thaw, rinse, and squeeze the excess liquid from the spinach.

4. Place the cooked or thawed spinach in a medium bowl. Add all of the remaining ingredients, and mix well. Serve at room temperature.

Per serving: Calories: 28, Protein: 1 g, Fat: 2 g, Carbohydrates: 2 g

SPICY BEAN SPROUTS
KONGNAMUL MUCHIM

Yield: 4 servings

4 cups water
½ teaspoon salt
½ pound soybean sprouts
1 tablespoon soy sauce
1 teaspoon white vinegar
1 teaspoon sugar
1 teaspoon gochujang (see glossary, p. 6)
2 green onions, green and white parts, minced

1. In a large pan, heat the water to boiling. Add the salt and bean sprouts. Parboil the sprouts until they are pliant yet crisp, about 1 minute. Remove from the heat and place in a colander. Rinse the sprouts in cold water. Drain thoroughly and place in a medium bowl.

2. In a small bowl, thoroughly mix the soy sauce, vinegar, sugar, and gochujang. Add the onions.

3. Pour this mixture over the bean sprouts, and gently toss. Serve immediately.

Per serving: Calories: 25, Protein: 2 g, Fat: 0 g, Carbohydrates: 5 g

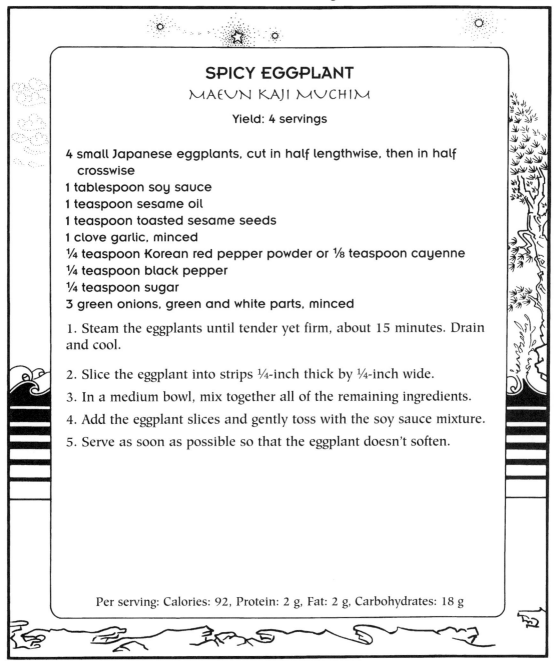

SPICY EGGPLANT

MAEUN KAJI MUCHIM

Yield: 4 servings

4 small Japanese eggplants, cut in half lengthwise, then in half crosswise
1 tablespoon soy sauce
1 teaspoon sesame oil
1 teaspoon toasted sesame seeds
1 clove garlic, minced
¼ teaspoon Korean red pepper powder or ⅛ teaspoon cayenne
¼ teaspoon black pepper
¼ teaspoon sugar
3 green onions, green and white parts, minced

1. Steam the eggplants until tender yet firm, about 15 minutes. Drain and cool.

2. Slice the eggplant into strips ¼-inch thick by ¼-inch wide.

3. In a medium bowl, mix together all of the remaining ingredients.

4. Add the eggplant slices and gently toss with the soy sauce mixture.

5. Serve as soon as possible so that the eggplant doesn't soften.

Per serving: Calories: 92, Protein: 2 g, Fat: 2 g, Carbohydrates: 18 g

SPICY MUSHROOMS

MAEUN BOSOT SANGCHAE

Yield: 2 main-dish servings or 4 side-dish servings

A mushroom lovers' delight. Choose your favorite mushroom variety for flavor and texture, then combine with the bite of green chili and garlic for a personalized side dish.

1 cup dried mushrooms (Dried black and shiitake mushrooms make a tasty combination.)
1 small green chili pepper, seeded and thinly sliced
2 cloves garlic, minced
2 tablespoons soy sauce
1 tablespoon sugar
1 teaspoon cider vinegar
1 teaspoon salt
½ teaspoon pepper
2 tablespoons vegetable oil

1. Wash the mushrooms in cool water, then cover with fresh water and allow to soak for 1 hour. Drain and dry. Cut the stems off and discard. Cut the caps into ¼-inch wide strips.

2. Place all the ingredients except the oil in a large bowl. Mix thoroughly and let stand for 10 minutes.

3. In a wok or large skillet, heat the oil over medium-high heat. Add the mushroom mixture. Stir-fry until the liquid is absorbed, about 3 minutes.

4. Serve with rice or noodles.

Per 3 servings: Calories: 146, Protein: 3 g, Fat: 9 g, Carbohydrates: 13 g

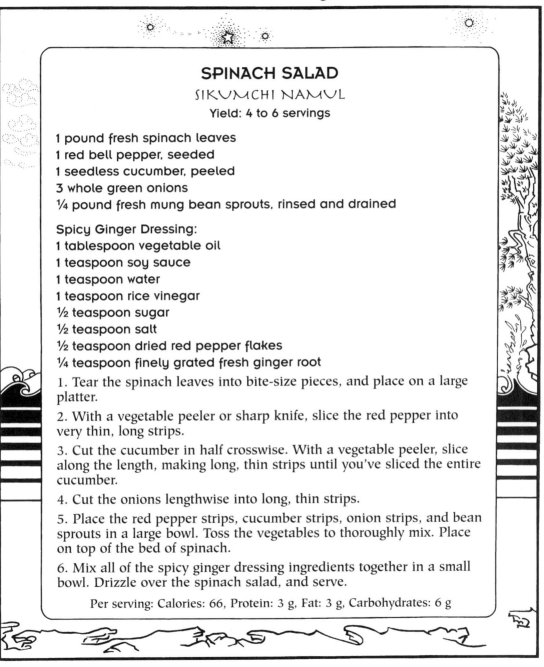

SPINACH SALAD
SIKUMCHI NAMUL
Yield: 4 to 6 servings

1 pound fresh spinach leaves
1 red bell pepper, seeded
1 seedless cucumber, peeled
3 whole green onions
¼ pound fresh mung bean sprouts, rinsed and drained

Spicy Ginger Dressing:
1 tablespoon vegetable oil
1 teaspoon soy sauce
1 teaspoon water
1 teaspoon rice vinegar
½ teaspoon sugar
½ teaspoon salt
½ teaspoon dried red pepper flakes
¼ teaspoon finely grated fresh ginger root

1. Tear the spinach leaves into bite-size pieces, and place on a large platter.

2. With a vegetable peeler or sharp knife, slice the red pepper into very thin, long strips.

3. Cut the cucumber in half crosswise. With a vegetable peeler, slice along the length, making long, thin strips until you've sliced the entire cucumber.

4. Cut the onions lengthwise into long, thin strips.

5. Place the red pepper strips, cucumber strips, onion strips, and bean sprouts in a large bowl. Toss the vegetables to thoroughly mix. Place on top of the bed of spinach.

6. Mix all of the spicy ginger dressing ingredients together in a small bowl. Drizzle over the spinach salad, and serve.

Per serving: Calories: 66, Protein: 3 g, Fat: 3 g, Carbohydrates: 6 g

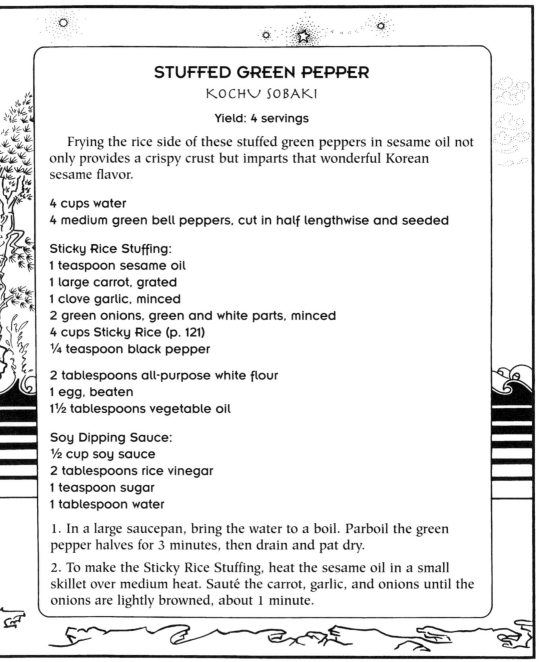

STUFFED GREEN PEPPER

KOCHU SOBAKI

Yield: 4 servings

Frying the rice side of these stuffed green peppers in sesame oil not only provides a crispy crust but imparts that wonderful Korean sesame flavor.

4 cups water
4 medium green bell peppers, cut in half lengthwise and seeded

Sticky Rice Stuffing:
1 teaspoon sesame oil
1 large carrot, grated
1 clove garlic, minced
2 green onions, green and white parts, minced
4 cups Sticky Rice (p. 121)
¼ teaspoon black pepper

2 tablespoons all-purpose white flour
1 egg, beaten
1½ tablespoons vegetable oil

Soy Dipping Sauce:
½ cup soy sauce
2 tablespoons rice vinegar
1 teaspoon sugar
1 tablespoon water

1. In a large saucepan, bring the water to a boil. Parboil the green pepper halves for 3 minutes, then drain and pat dry.

2. To make the Sticky Rice Stuffing, heat the sesame oil in a small skillet over medium heat. Sauté the carrot, garlic, and onions until the onions are lightly browned, about 1 minute.

3. In a medium bowl, mix the carrot mixture with the Sticky Rice, salt, and pepper.

4. Fill each pepper half with ½ cup of the stuffing mixture, pressing firmly.

5. Dip the stuffed side of each pepper half into the flour and then into the beaten egg.

6. In a large skillet, heat the vegetable oil over medium heat. Place the peppers in the skillet stuffing-side down, and fry until golden brown and crispy.

7. To make the Soy Dipping Sauce, mix all the ingredients together in a small bowl.

8. Serve the stuffed peppers on a large serving platter along with the bowl of dipping sauce.

Per serving: Calories: 191, Protein: 6 g, Fat: 7 g, Carbohydrates: 23 g

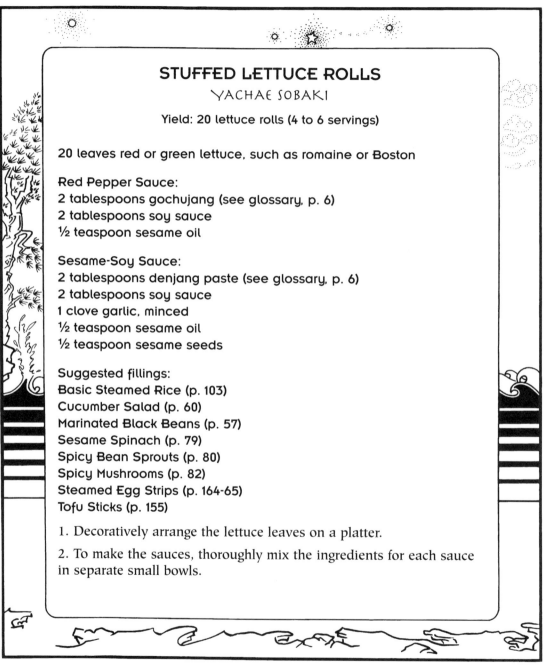

STUFFED LETTUCE ROLLS

YACHAE SOBAKI

Yield: 20 lettuce rolls (4 to 6 servings)

20 leaves red or green lettuce, such as romaine or Boston

Red Pepper Sauce:
2 tablespoons gochujang (see glossary, p. 6)
2 tablespoons soy sauce
½ teaspoon sesame oil

Sesame-Soy Sauce:
2 tablespoons denjang paste (see glossary, p. 6)
2 tablespoons soy sauce
1 clove garlic, minced
½ teaspoon sesame oil
½ teaspoon sesame seeds

Suggested fillings:
Basic Steamed Rice (p. 103)
Cucumber Salad (p. 60)
Marinated Black Beans (p. 57)
Sesame Spinach (p. 79)
Spicy Bean Sprouts (p. 80)
Spicy Mushrooms (p. 82)
Steamed Egg Strips (p. 164-65)
Tofu Sticks (p. 155)

1. Decoratively arrange the lettuce leaves on a platter.

2. To make the sauces, thoroughly mix the ingredients for each sauce in separate small bowls.

3. Place the sauce bowls on two large platters. Arrange the various fillings on the two platters surrounding the bowls.

4. To assemble the lettuce rolls, each person spreads the sauce of his/her choice on a lettuce leaf, fills it with a filling, then folds the leaf over the filling, and rolls it into a cigar shape. Dip the rolls into the sauces.

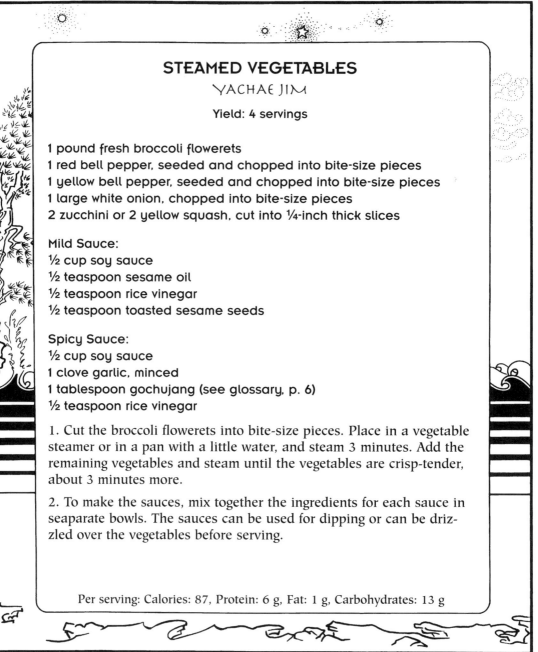

STEAMED VEGETABLES
YACHAE JIM

Yield: 4 servings

1 pound fresh broccoli flowerets
1 red bell pepper, seeded and chopped into bite-size pieces
1 yellow bell pepper, seeded and chopped into bite-size pieces
1 large white onion, chopped into bite-size pieces
2 zucchini or 2 yellow squash, cut into ¼-inch thick slices

Mild Sauce:
½ cup soy sauce
½ teaspoon sesame oil
½ teaspoon rice vinegar
½ teaspoon toasted sesame seeds

Spicy Sauce:
½ cup soy sauce
1 clove garlic, minced
1 tablespoon gochujang (see glossary, p. 6)
½ teaspoon rice vinegar

1. Cut the broccoli flowerets into bite-size pieces. Place in a vegetable steamer or in a pan with a little water, and steam 3 minutes. Add the remaining vegetables and steam until the vegetables are crisp-tender, about 3 minutes more.

2. To make the sauces, mix together the ingredients for each sauce in seaparate bowls. The sauces can be used for dipping or can be drizzled over the vegetables before serving.

Per serving: Calories: 87, Protein: 6 g, Fat: 1 g, Carbohydrates: 13 g

SWEET POTATO PANCAKES

KOKUMA JON

Yield: 1 dozen pancakes (4 to 6 servings)

Sweet Potato Pancakes are a combination of two Korean favorites—sweet potatoes and pancakes. The dipping sauce adds the Korean spunk. This makes a tasty treat for lunch.

1 large sweet potato, peeled, cooked, and mashed
1 egg, beaten
¾ cup all-purpose white flour
½ teaspoon salt
1¼ cups water
3 green onions, green and white parts, chopped
Vegetable oil for frying

Dipping Sauce:
½ cup soy sauce
1 teaspoon rice vinegar
¼ teaspoon grated fresh ginger root
¼ teaspoon sesame oil

1. In a medium bowl, mix the mashed sweet potato, egg, flour, salt, and water. Add the onions and stir to mix.

2. Lightly coat a large skillet or electric frypan with vegetable oil. Heat to 350 degrees or medium-high heat. Ladle ¼ cup of the batter into the skillet. With a spatula or the back of a spoon, spread the batter into a thin 3-inch circle. Cook until the edges turn golden brown and bubbles form, about 2 or 3 minutes. With a spatula, flip the pancake and cook the other side for 2 minutes more. Repeat until all the batter has been used.

3. Mix the dipping sauce ingredients together in a small bowl. Place the bowl of dipping sauce and the sweet potato pancakes on a large platter, and serve.

Per pancake: Calories: 191, Protein: 6 g, Fat: 7 g, Carbohydrates: 23 g

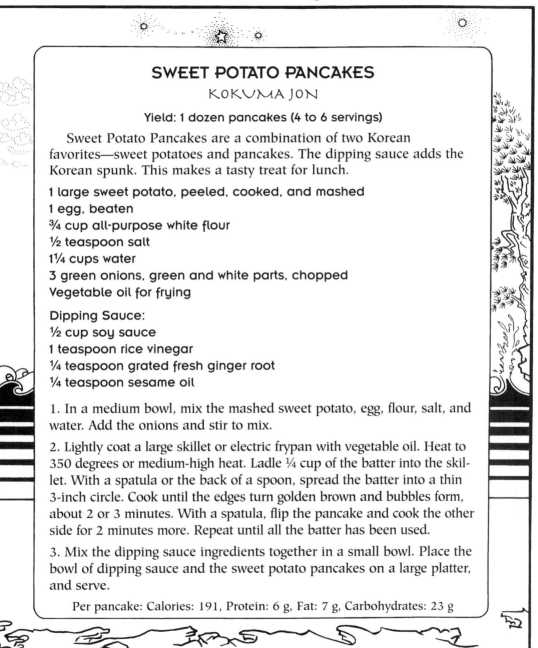

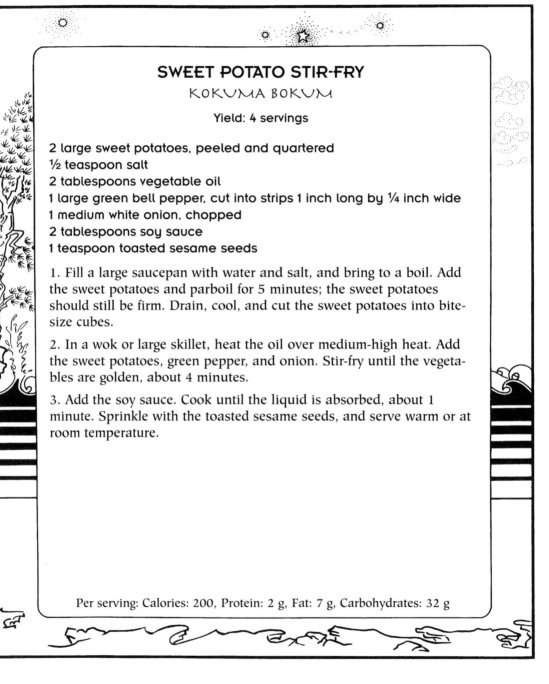

SWEET POTATO STIR-FRY

KOKUMA BOKUM

Yield: 4 servings

2 large sweet potatoes, peeled and quartered
½ teaspoon salt
2 tablespoons vegetable oil
1 large green bell pepper, cut into strips 1 inch long by ¼ inch wide
1 medium white onion, chopped
2 tablespoons soy sauce
1 teaspoon toasted sesame seeds

1. Fill a large saucepan with water and salt, and bring to a boil. Add the sweet potatoes and parboil for 5 minutes; the sweet potatoes should still be firm. Drain, cool, and cut the sweet potatoes into bite-size cubes.

2. In a wok or large skillet, heat the oil over medium-high heat. Add the sweet potatoes, green pepper, and onion. Stir-fry until the vegetables are golden, about 4 minutes.

3. Add the soy sauce. Cook until the liquid is absorbed, about 1 minute. Sprinkle with the toasted sesame seeds, and serve warm or at room temperature.

Per serving: Calories: 200, Protein: 2 g, Fat: 7 g, Carbohydrates: 32 g

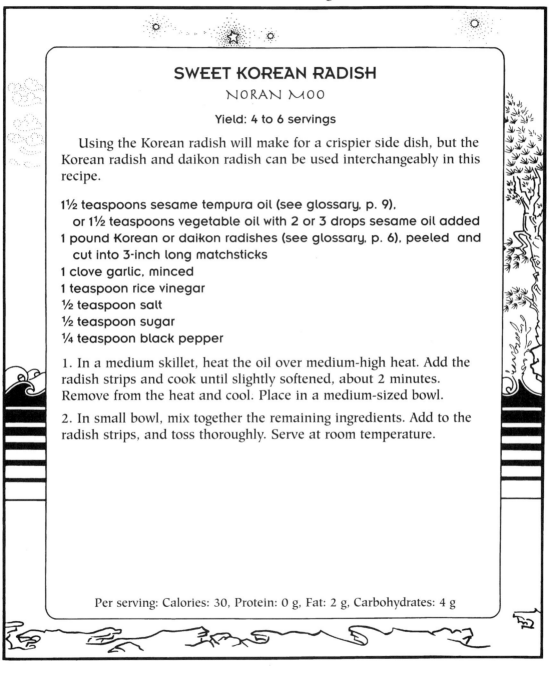

SWEET KOREAN RADISH

NORAN MOO

Yield: 4 to 6 servings

Using the Korean radish will make for a crispier side dish, but the Korean radish and daikon radish can be used interchangeably in this recipe.

1½ teaspoons sesame tempura oil (see glossary, p. 9),
   or 1½ teaspoons vegetable oil with 2 or 3 drops sesame oil added
1 pound Korean or daikon radishes (see glossary, p. 6), peeled and
   cut into 3-inch long matchsticks
1 clove garlic, minced
1 teaspoon rice vinegar
½ teaspoon salt
½ teaspoon sugar
¼ teaspoon black pepper

1. In a medium skillet, heat the oil over medium-high heat. Add the radish strips and cook until slightly softened, about 2 minutes. Remove from the heat and cool. Place in a medium-sized bowl.

2. In small bowl, mix together the remaining ingredients. Add to the radish strips, and toss thoroughly. Serve at room temperature.

Per serving: Calories: 30, Protein: 0 g, Fat: 2 g, Carbohydrates: 4 g

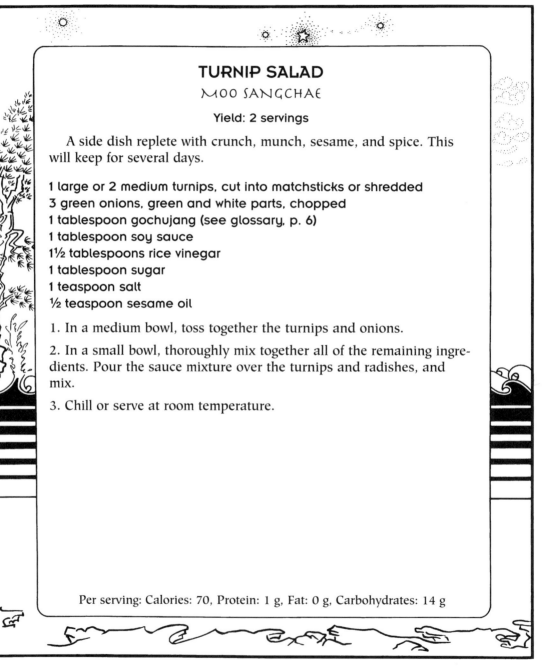

TURNIP SALAD

MOO SANGCHAE

Yield: 2 servings

A side dish replete with crunch, munch, sesame, and spice. This will keep for several days.

1 large or 2 medium turnips, cut into matchsticks or shredded
3 green onions, green and white parts, chopped
1 tablespoon gochujang (see glossary, p. 6)
1 tablespoon soy sauce
1½ tablespoons rice vinegar
1 tablespoon sugar
1 teaspoon salt
½ teaspoon sesame oil

1. In a medium bowl, toss together the turnips and onions.

2. In a small bowl, thoroughly mix together all of the remaining ingredients. Pour the sauce mixture over the turnips and radishes, and mix.

3. Chill or serve at room temperature.

Per serving: Calories: 70, Protein: 1 g, Fat: 0 g, Carbohydrates: 14 g

VEGETABLE STIR-FRY

YACHAE BOKUM

Yield: 4 servings

1½ tablespoons vegetable oil
1 small Chinese cabbage, shredded
2 carrots, shredded
4 green onions, green and white parts, chopped
1 red bell pepper, cut into matchsticks
1 medium zucchini, cut into matchsticks
½ pound firm tofu, rinsed, drained, and cut into cubes
2 tablespoons soy sauce
1 teaspoon rice vinegar
½ tablespoon toasted sesame seeds

1. In a large wok, heat the oil over high heat. Add the cabbage and stir-fry for 2 minutes. Add the remaining vegetables and tofu, and fry 2 minutes more.

2. Add the soy sauce and rice vinegar, and cook until the moisture is absorbed, about 1 minute more. Transfer to a serving platter.

3. Sprinkle with the toasted sesame seeds. Serve with rice or noodles.

Per serving: Calories: 135, Protein: 6 g, Fat: 8 g, Carbohydrates: 10 g

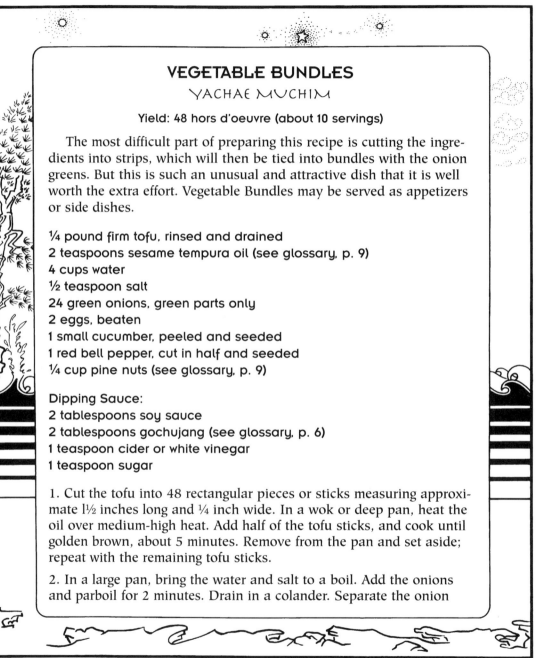

VEGETABLE BUNDLES
YACHAE MUCHIM

Yield: 48 hors d'oeuvre (about 10 servings)

The most difficult part of preparing this recipe is cutting the ingredients into strips, which will then be tied into bundles with the onion greens. But this is such an unusual and attractive dish that it is well worth the extra effort. Vegetable Bundles may be served as appetizers or side dishes.

¼ pound firm tofu, rinsed and drained
2 teaspoons sesame tempura oil (see glossary, p. 9)
4 cups water
½ teaspoon salt
24 green onions, green parts only
2 eggs, beaten
1 small cucumber, peeled and seeded
1 red bell pepper, cut in half and seeded
¼ cup pine nuts (see glossary, p. 9)

Dipping Sauce:
2 tablespoons soy sauce
2 tablespoons gochujang (see glossary, p. 6)
1 teaspoon cider or white vinegar
1 teaspoon sugar

1. Cut the tofu into 48 rectangular pieces or sticks measuring approximate 1½ inches long and ¼ inch wide. In a wok or deep pan, heat the oil over medium-high heat. Add half of the tofu sticks, and cook until golden brown, about 5 minutes. Remove from the pan and set aside; repeat with the remaining tofu sticks.

2. In a large pan, bring the water and salt to a boil. Add the onions and parboil for 2 minutes. Drain in a colander. Separate the onion

greens so that you have at least 48 onion strips, and set aside on a towel to soak up any excess water.

3. In a large skillet, heat the remaining 1 teaspoon of oil over medium-high heat. Add the eggs, shaping them into a rectangle about 8 inches by 6 inches. Cook until firm. Slide onto a cutting board, and cool. Cut into 48 rectangular shapes the same size as the tofu pieces. Set aside.

4. Cut the cucumber and red pepper into 48 rectangles the same size as the egg and tofu pieces.

5. To assemble the bundles, place one green onion strip flat on a cutting board. Layer a tofu strip, egg strip, cucumber strip, and red pepper strip on the onion. Lift the ends of the green onion around the stack of strips, and tie a snug knot over the layers. Snip off any excess length of green onion with kitchen shears.

7. Tuck 1 or 2 pine nuts in the center of each vegetable bundle.

8. Mix the dipping sauce ingredients together in a small bowl.

9. Place the bowl of dipping sauce in the center of a large platter. Arrange the vegetable bundles around the bowl of dipping sauce, and serve.

Per serving: Calories: 14, Protein: 1 g, Fat: 0 g, Carbohydrates: 1 g

VEGETABLE PANCAKES

YACHAE JON

Yield: Makes approximately 1½ dozen pancakes (4 servings)

The rice flour used in these pancakes provides a chewier pancake, and the fresh vegetables impart not only flavor but a bit of crunch.

½ teaspoon sesame oil
1 small carrot, grated
½ green bell pepper, minced
2 green onions, green and white parts, minced

Batter:
¾ cup all-purpose white flour
¼ cup rice flour
1 egg
½ teaspoon salt
1 cup water

Vegetable oil for frying

Dipping Sauce:
¼ cup soy sauce
½ teaspoon rice vinegar
¼ teaspoon sesame seeds

1. In a small skillet, heat the sesame oil over medium-high heat. Add the carrot, green pepper, and onions, and stir-fry for 1 minute. Remove from the heat and cool.

2. Mix the batter ingredients together in a medium bowl. The consistency should be fairly thin. If too thick, add more water.

3. Add the cooled vegetables to the batter, and gently stir.

4. In a small skillet (preferably nonstick), place ½ teaspoon of vegetable oil, and heat to medium or medium-high heat. Ladle about ¼ cup of the vegetable batter into the skillet. Tilt the pan so that the batter spreads into a 3-inch circle. Cook until the edges turn golden brown, about 1 minute. With a spatula, flip the pancake and cook the other side for 1 minute more. Repeat until all the batter has been used.

5. Mix the dipping sauce ingredients together in a small bowl. Place the bowl of dipping sauce and the vegetable pancakes on a large platter, and serve.

Per pancake: Calories: 37, Protein: 2 g, Fat: 0 g, Carbohydrates: 6 g

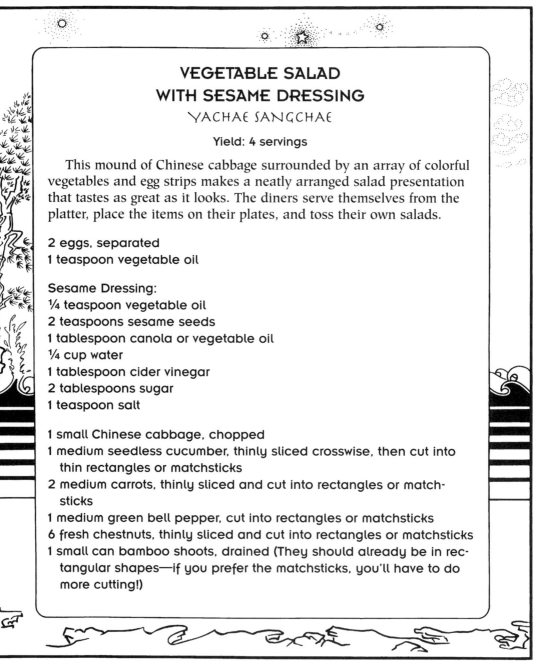

VEGETABLE SALAD
WITH SESAME DRESSING
YACHAE SANGCHAE

Yield: 4 servings

This mound of Chinese cabbage surrounded by an array of colorful vegetables and egg strips makes a neatly arranged salad presentation that tastes as great as it looks. The diners serve themselves from the platter, place the items on their plates, and toss their own salads.

2 eggs, separated
1 teaspoon vegetable oil

Sesame Dressing:
¼ teaspoon vegetable oil
2 teaspoons sesame seeds
1 tablespoon canola or vegetable oil
¼ cup water
1 tablespoon cider vinegar
2 tablespoons sugar
1 teaspoon salt

1 small Chinese cabbage, chopped
1 medium seedless cucumber, thinly sliced crosswise, then cut into
   thin rectangles or matchsticks
2 medium carrots, thinly sliced and cut into rectangles or matchsticks
1 medium green bell pepper, cut into rectangles or matchsticks
6 fresh chestnuts, thinly sliced and cut into rectangles or matchsticks
1 small can bamboo shoots, drained (They should already be in rectangular shapes—if you prefer the matchsticks, you'll have to do
   more cutting!)

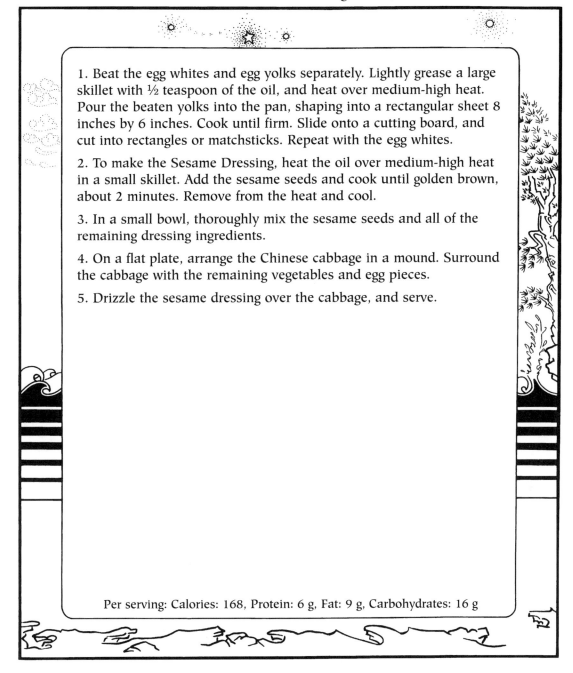

1. Beat the egg whites and egg yolks separately. Lightly grease a large skillet with ½ teaspoon of the oil, and heat over medium-high heat. Pour the beaten yolks into the pan, shaping into a rectangular sheet 8 inches by 6 inches. Cook until firm. Slide onto a cutting board, and cut into rectangles or matchsticks. Repeat with the egg whites.

2. To make the Sesame Dressing, heat the oil over medium-high heat in a small skillet. Add the sesame seeds and cook until golden brown, about 2 minutes. Remove from the heat and cool.

3. In a small bowl, thoroughly mix the sesame seeds and all of the remaining dressing ingredients.

4. On a flat plate, arrange the Chinese cabbage in a mound. Surround the cabbage with the remaining vegetables and egg pieces.

5. Drizzle the sesame dressing over the cabbage, and serve.

Per serving: Calories: 168, Protein: 6 g, Fat: 9 g, Carbohydrates: 16 g

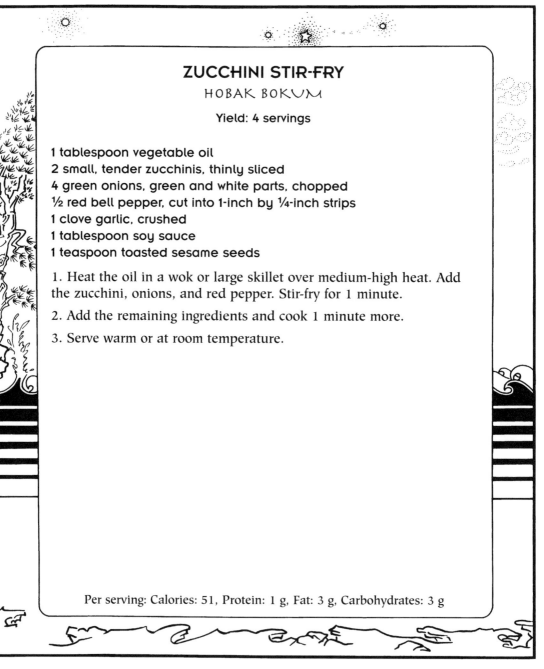

ZUCCHINI STIR-FRY

HOBAK BOKUM

Yield: 4 servings

1 tablespoon vegetable oil
2 small, tender zucchinis, thinly sliced
4 green onions, green and white parts, chopped
½ red bell pepper, cut into 1-inch by ¼-inch strips
1 clove garlic, crushed
1 tablespoon soy sauce
1 teaspoon toasted sesame seeds

1. Heat the oil in a wok or large skillet over medium-high heat. Add the zucchini, onions, and red pepper. Stir-fry for 1 minute.

2. Add the remaining ingredients and cook 1 minute more.

3. Serve warm or at room temperature.

Per serving: Calories: 51, Protein: 1 g, Fat: 3 g, Carbohydrates: 3 g

Rice Dishes

BAP

Rice is a staple of Korean cuisine and is served at almost every meal. Not only does it serve as a buffer for some of the spicier foods, but it's also filling and low in fat. Medium-grain white rice seems to be the preference of most Korean cooks, and large bags of this type of rice can be purchased in Asian markets and most large grocery stores. The rice is cooked to a somewhat sticky consistency; the grains of rice are shiny and hold their shape. One way to ensure the right consistency is to use a rice cooker. Just remember to measure accurately, and the rice will turn out perfect every time.

BASIC STEAMED RICE

BAP

Yield: Four 1-cup servings

A bowl of medium-grain white rice can almost always be found on a Korean table. It serves to temper the fire in some of the spicier dishes.

1½ cups medium-grain white rice
2 cups water

1. In a medium pan, combine the rice and water, and bring to a boil. Reduce the heat to a simmer, and cover. Simmer until the liquid is absorbed, about 20 minutes.

2. Remove the pan from the heat. Let set for about 10 minutes, then stir the rice.

3. Serve warm or use the rice in other recipes.

Per serving: Calories: 158, Protein: 3 g, Fat: 0 g, Carbohydrates: 35 g

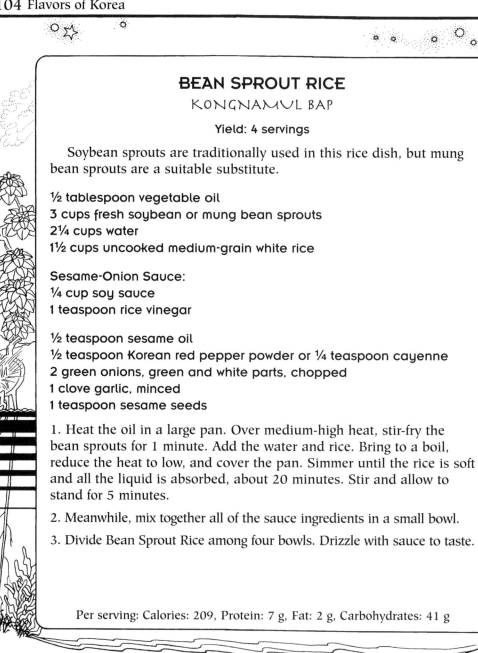

BEAN SPROUT RICE

KONGNAMUL BAP

Yield: 4 servings

Soybean sprouts are traditionally used in this rice dish, but mung bean sprouts are a suitable substitute.

½ tablespoon vegetable oil
3 cups fresh soybean or mung bean sprouts
2¼ cups water
1½ cups uncooked medium-grain white rice

Sesame-Onion Sauce:
¼ cup soy sauce
1 teaspoon rice vinegar

½ teaspoon sesame oil
½ teaspoon Korean red pepper powder or ¼ teaspoon cayenne
2 green onions, green and white parts, chopped
1 clove garlic, minced
1 teaspoon sesame seeds

1. Heat the oil in a large pan. Over medium-high heat, stir-fry the bean sprouts for 1 minute. Add the water and rice. Bring to a boil, reduce the heat to low, and cover the pan. Simmer until the rice is soft and all the liquid is absorbed, about 20 minutes. Stir and allow to stand for 5 minutes.

2. Meanwhile, mix together all of the sauce ingredients in a small bowl.

3. Divide Bean Sprout Rice among four bowls. Drizzle with sauce to taste.

Per serving: Calories: 209, Protein: 7 g, Fat: 2 g, Carbohydrates: 41 g

BROCCOLI RICE
YACHAE BAP

Yield: 4 generous servings

1 tablespoon vegetable oil
2 cups broccoli, cut into bite-size pieces
6 green onions, green and white parts, chopped
2 cloves garlic, minced
4 cups cooked rice
½ tablespoon sesame tempura oil (see glossary, p. 9), or vegetable oil plus 2 drops sesame oil 2 eggs, beaten
1 tablespoon soy sauce
¼ to ½ teaspoon Korean red pepper powder or ¼ to ⅛ teaspoon cayenne
½ teaspoon salt
¼ teaspoon black pepper

1. In a wok or large skillet, heat the oil to about 350 degrees, or until hot but not smoking. Add the broccoli and cook until crisp tender, about 5 minutes.

2. Add the onions and cook until golden brown, about 2 minutes.

3. Add the garlic and rice, and cook 2 minutes more, stirring constantly.

4. Push the rice-broccoli mixture to one side of the wok or skillet, and add the sesame oil to the pan. Cook the eggs in the oil, and, when firm, stir the cooked eggs into the rice-broccoli mixture.

5. Add the soy sauce, Korean red pepper powder, salt, and pepper. Cook, stirring, until all liquid is absorbed (about 2 minutes), then serve.

Per serving: Calories: 251, Protein: 6 g, Fat: 7 g, Carbohydrates: 38 g

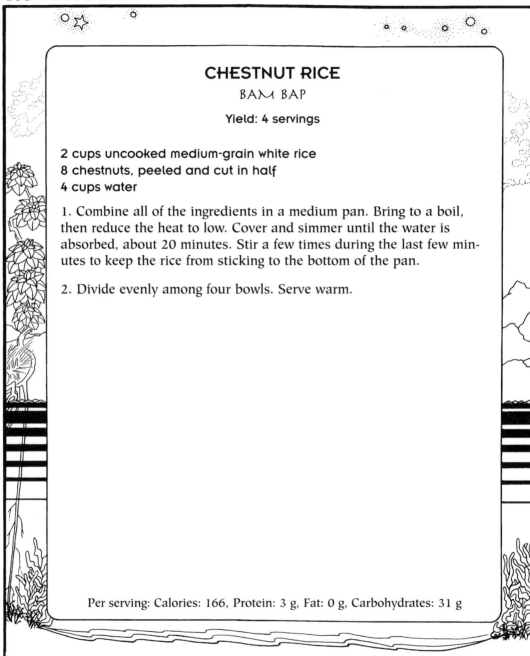

CHESTNUT RICE
BAM BAP

Yield: 4 servings

2 cups uncooked medium-grain white rice
8 chestnuts, peeled and cut in half
4 cups water

1. Combine all of the ingredients in a medium pan. Bring to a boil, then reduce the heat to low. Cover and simmer until the water is absorbed, about 20 minutes. Stir a few times during the last few minutes to keep the rice from sticking to the bottom of the pan.

2. Divide evenly among four bowls. Serve warm.

Per serving: Calories: 166, Protein: 3 g, Fat: 0 g, Carbohydrates: 31 g

FRIED RICE (MILD)

YACHAE BOKUM BAP

Yield: 4 to 6 servings

Fried rice is Chinese in origin, but we have included some recipes that our friends and families have enjoyed.

1½ tablespoons vegetable oil
2 stalks celery, cut in half lengthwise, then thinly sliced crosswise
½ white onion, chopped
½ red bell pepper, chopped
3 green onions, green and white parts, chopped
2 cloves garlic, minced
2 eggs, beaten
4 cups cooked rice
2 tablespoons soy sauce
½ teaspoon salt
¼ teaspoon pepper

1. In a wok or large skillet, heat the oil to 375 degrees, or until hot but not smoking. Add the celery, onion, red pepper, onions, and garlic. Stir-fry for 2 minutes.

2. Push the vegetables aside in the wok or pan, and add the eggs. Cook the eggs for 1 minute, stirring constantly.

3. Add the cooked rice and soy sauce to the eggs and vegetables. Stir-fry until the moisture is absorbed, about 2 minutes.

4. Season with salt and pepper. Serve warm.

Per serving: Calories: 202, Protein: 5 g, Fat: 6 g, Carbohydrates: 31 g

FIERY FRIED RICE

BOKUM BAP

Yield: 4 servings

This is a spicy version of fried rice. It's been blessed with those celebrated Korean seasonings—chili pepper and sesame.

1½ tablespoons sesame tempura oil (see glossary, p. 9), or vegetable oil with 2 drops sesame chili oil added
8 dried red chili peppers
5 green onions, green and white parts, chopped
2 cloves garlic, minced
1 cup coarsely shredded cabbage
2 eggs, beaten
4 cups cooked rice
2 tablespoons soy sauce
¼ teaspoon Korean red pepper powder or ⅛ teaspoon cayenne
Salt and pepper, to taste

1. In a wok or large skillet, heat the oil over medium-high heat. Add the chili peppers, onions, garlic, and cabbage. Stir-fry for 1 minute.

2. Push the vegetables to one side of the pan. Pour in the beaten eggs, stirring to break them up as they cook.

3. Add the rice and stir-fry for 1 minute.

4. Add in the soy sauce and red pepper powder. Cook until the moisture is absorbed, about 1 or 2 minutes. Add salt and pepper to taste.

Per serving: Calories: 285, Protein: 8 g, Fat: 7 g, Carbohydrates: 45 g

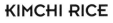

KIMCHI RICE

KIMCHI BAP

Yield: 4 servings

Kimchi rice is traditionally made with cabbage kimchi (pickled cabbage), but there is no reason that an adventurous cook can't experiment with some of the other vegetable kimchis to create his or her own personalized and unique dish.

2 teaspoons sesame oil
2 cups cabbage kimchi (p. 36), drained and chopped (reserve the liquid)
Reserved kimchi liquid plus water to equal 2 cups
1½ cups uncooked medium-grain white rice

Garlic-Soy Sauce:
¼ cup soy sauce
1 clove garlic, crushed
1 green onion, minced
Toasted sesame seeds

Garnish:
2 hard-boiled eggs, sliced
4 Sesame Seaweed Squares (p. 78), cut into narrow strips

1. Heat the oil in a deep pan over medium-high heat. Fry the kimchi for 1 minute. Add the kimchi liquid and water, and stir in the rice. Reduce the heat to low, and cook until the liquid has been absorbed, about 20 minutes. Stir the rice and remove from the heat.

2. In a small bowl, mix the sauce ingredients together.

3. Place the kimchi rice in individual bowls. Garnish with the egg slices and seaweed strips. Serve warm with the sauce.

Per serving: Calories: 229, Protein: 7 g, Fat: 5 g, Carbohydrates: 37 g

OMELET RICE

GERAN BOKUM BAP

Yield: 1 serving

Mushroom-Rice Filling:
½ teaspoon vegetable oil
1 green onion, green and white parts, chopped
2 fresh button mushrooms, chopped
½ cup cooked medium-grain white rice
Salt and pepper, to taste

Red Pepper Sauce:
2 tablespoons soy sauce
1 tablespoon gochujang (see glossary, p. 6)
½ teaspoon rice vinegar
½ teaspoon sugar

Omelet:
1 teaspoon water
2 eggs, beaten
½ teaspoon vegetable oil

1. To make the filling, heat the oil in a small skillet. Over medium-high heat, stir-fry the onion and mushrooms for 1 minute. Add the rice, salt, and pepper, and cook 1 minute more. Set aside.

2. Mix the sauce ingredients in a small bowl.

3. To make the omelet, add the water to the eggs, and stir. In a small nonstick skillet or omelet pan, heat the oil over medium-high heat. Add the eggs, tilting the pan so that the egg mixture spreads evenly over the bottom of the pan. When the eggs are set (after about 1 minute), loosen the omelet from the pan with a spatula. Spread the rice mixture over half of the omelet. Fold the other half over the top. Transfer to a plate, and serve with the sauce.

Per serving: Calories: 281, Protein: 14 g, Fat: 12 g, Carbohydrates: 25 g

POTATO FRIED RICE

KAMJA BOKUM BAP

Yield: 4 servings

1½ tablespoons vegetable oil
2 potatoes, cooked, peeled, and diced
1 carrot, coarsely shredded
4 green onions, green and white parts, chopped
2 cloves garlic, minced
2 eggs, beaten
3 cups cooked rice
2 tablespoons soy sauce
Salt and pepper, to taste

1. In a wok or large skillet, heat the oil. Over medium-high heat, stir-fry the potatoes, carrot, onions, and garlic for 1 minute.

2. Push the vegetables to one side of the wok or skillet, and add the eggs. Cook the eggs, stirring, until they are firm, about 1 minute.

3. Add the rice, soy sauce, salt, and pepper, and mix well. Cook 1 minute more. Serve warm.

Per serving: Calories: 300, Protein: 7 g, Fat: 7 g, Carbohydrates: 51 g

RICE BALLS
SAM BAP

Yield: 1½ dozen balls (4 to 6 servings)

A versatile dish, rice balls with vegetable fillings may be served as a snack or party hors d'oeuvre along with this dipping sauce. Rice balls with fruit fillings can be rolled in sugar and served as a dessert.

2 cups water
1½ cups uncooked medium-grain white rice
½ teaspoon salt
1 tablespoon rice vinegar
2 tablespoons sugar

Suggested fillings:
Any type of fruit cut into ½-inch pieces
Dates, cut into halves or thirds
Seedless cucumber, cut into ½-inch pieces
Sweet potato, cooked and cut into ½-inch pieces

½ cup pine nuts or chestnuts, crushed

Dipping Sauce:
¼ cup soy sauce
¼ teaspoon Korean red pepper powder or ⅛ teaspoon cayenne
1 green onion, minced

1. In a medium pan, heat the water, rice, and salt to boiling. Reduce the heat to low, and simmer until the liquid is absorbed, about 20 minutes.

2. After the rice is cooked and still warm, add the rice vinegar and sugar. Mix thoroughly. Scoop up 1 heaping tablespoon of rice, place a piece of one of the suggested fillings in the center of the rice, and form

a ball around the filling. (It's easier to form the rice ball if the rice is warm and your hands are wet.) While the rice balls are still moist, roll them in the crushed pine nuts or chestnuts.

3. Mix the dipping sauce ingredients in a small bowl.

4. Serve the rice balls and dipping sauce at room temperature.

Per rice ball without filling:
Calories: 66, Protein: 2 g, Fat: 2 g, Carbohydrates: 10 gm

RED BEANS AND RICE
PAT BAP

Yield: 4 main-dish servings or 6 side-dish servings

Red soybeans—also known as Asian red beans—along with red pepper powder give this dish an interesting pinkish tint. Even though there is red pepper powder and color in this dish, it's still fairly mild tasting.

3½ cups water
⅓ cup dried red soybeans (Asian red beans), rinsed
2 cups uncooked medium-grain white rice
½ teaspoon Korean red pepper powder or ¼ teaspoon cayenne
½ teaspoon salt

1. In a medium pan, bring the water and beans to a boil. Cover and reduce the heat to simmer. Cook until the beans are soft, about 1 hour. Drain the beans, reserving the liquid.

2. In a large pan, add the bean liquid plus enough water to equal 4 cups. Bring to a boil. Add the beans and all of the remaining ingredients. Cover and reduce the heat to simmer. Cook until the rice is soft, about 20 minutes, then serve.

Per 4 servings: Calories: 217, Protein: 6 g, Fat: 0 g, Carbohydrates: 46 g

RICE CAKES WITH VEGETABLES

YACHAE DOK BOKUM

Yield: 2 main-dish servings or 4 side-dish servings

If you have never tried rice cakes, this is a wonderful introduction to their versatility and ability to absorb flavors. They have a chewy texture, which contrasts to the other recipe ingredients, and they readily soak up the soy and sesame flavors.

4 large, dried shiitake mushrooms
2 cups firmly packed fresh spinach leaves, or one 10-ounce package
    frozen spinach, thawed and drained
2 tablespoons soy sauce
2 tablespoons sugar
4 green onions, green and white parts, chopped
2 cloves garlic, minced
½ cup water
2 tablespoons sesame oil
3 fresh rice cakes (about 8 inches in length), cut into ½-inch pieces
    (see glossary, p. 8)
2 medium carrots, thinly sliced

1. Soak the dried mushrooms in warm water to cover for 30 minutes. Drain and dry the mushrooms. Cut off the stems and discard. Slice the mushroom caps into thin strips.

2. In a medium saucepan, parboil the spinach in a little water for 2 minutes. Drain and squeeze out the excess water. With a knife or cooking scissors, cut the spinach into thirds crosswise.

3. In a small bowl, mix together the soy sauce, sugar, onions, garlic, and water.

4. In a large skillet or wok, heat the sesame oil. Fry the rice cakes, mushrooms, and carrots for about 2 minutes.

5. Add the soy sauce mixture, and simmer for 5 minutes.

6. Add the spinach and simmer 2 minutes more. Serve warm.

Per three: Calories: 334, Protein: 6 g, Fat: 9 g, Carbohydrates: 55 g

SPICY RICE CAKES
MAEUN DOK BOKUM

Yield: 2 main-dish or 4 side-dish servings

1 tablespoon sesame oil
½ cup diagonally sliced celery
1 carrot, thinly sliced on the diagonal
3 green onions, green and white parts, cut into 1-inch pieces
2 cups rice cakes (see glossary, p. 8), thinly sliced (¼-inch thick) on
    the diagonal
2 tablespoons soy sauce
1 tablespoon gochujang (see glossary, p. 6)
2 tablespoons sugar
2 tablespoons water

1. In a wok or large skillet, heat the oil over medium-high heat. Add the celery, carrot, and onions. Stir-fry for 1 minute.

2. Add the sliced rice cakes, and stir-fry 1 minute.

3. Add all of the remaining ingredients. Reduce the heat to low, and simmer for 5 minutes. Serve warm.

Per 2 servings: Calories: 244, Protein: 5 g, Fat: 7 g, Carbohydrates: 40 g

RICE WITH MIXED VEGETABLES
BIBIM BAP

Yield: 2 servings

Bibimbap is a classic Korean rice dish that must be tasted to be appreciated. Traditional bibimbap contains beef and seafood as well as vegetables, so if you order this dish in a Korean restaurant, make sure the cook eliminates the meat. If you get the chance to try this dish with the rice baked in the bowls (see the variation), take it. The crispy, sesame-flavored rice crust layered with crisp-tender vegetables is a treat to be savored.

2 large, dried shiitake mushrooms
2 teaspoons sesame tempura oil (see glossary, p. 9), or vegetable oil
    with 2 or 3 drops sesame oil added
½ seedless cucumber, cut into matchsticks
1 cup shredded Korean or daikon radish (see glossary, p. 6)
1 cup zucchini matchsticks
1 cup mung bean sprouts, blanched in boiling water for 1 minute and
    drained
2 eggs
2 cups cooked rice
Gochujang (see glossary, p. 6)

1. Soak the dried mushrooms in warm water to cover for 30 minutes. Drain and dry the mushrooms. Cut off the stems and discard. Slice the mushroom caps into thin strips.

2. In a small skillet, heat ½ teaspoon of the oil over medium-high heat. Fry the mushrooms for 1 minute. Remove from the heat and divide into two portions. Place each portion in the center of two deep oven-proof bowls. Place the two bowls in a warm oven (about 200 degrees) until all the vegetables and eggs are prepared.

3. In the same skillet, heat another ½ teaspoon oil. Fry the carrot for 1 minute. Remove from the heat and divide into two portions. Arrange each portion in a "wagon wheel" design with the mushrooms as the "hub" of the wheel. Place the two bowls back in the oven to keep the vegetables warm.

4. Repeat step 2 for the cucumber, radish, and zucchini. Arrange the vegetables and bean sprouts so that they fill in the "spokes" of the wagon wheel design.

5. In the skillet, add another ½ teaspoon oil. Over medium-high heat, fry each of the eggs sunnyside up. Place one egg on top of the mushrooms in each of the bowls.

6. The bowl of vegetables should be served warm along with a bowl of rice and a small dish of gochujang. Each diner can then mix the rice and gochujang with the vegetables according to their taste preference.

Variation: Another way of making bibimbap is to first mix the rice with 1½ teaspoons of sesame oil, and place the rice on the bottom and sides of a flame-proof clay pot or skillet with a cover. Layer the vegetables and eggs over the rice in the same "wagon-wheel" pattern. Cover the pot or skillet, and cook over moderate heat until the rice sizzles, about 2 to 3 minutes. This method creates a tasty rice crust, and the rice tends to take on a stronger vegetable flavor.

Per serving: Calories: 412, Protein: 12 g, Fat: 11 g, Carbohydrates: 63 g

SEAWEED RICE ROLLS
KIM BAP

Yield: 8 seaweed rolls (8 servings)

Kim bap is the Korean version of Japanese sushi; however, there's no raw fish or meat in these scrumptious seaweed treats. Kim bap can be served as an eye-catching and colorful appetizer or as a delectable side dish. Young remembers kim bap as a picnic food that her family would take along on outings in Korea. In fact, when Young and I took a cross-country trip, she packed a cooler full of kim bap. Unfortunately, the kim bap were so tasty that we had finished them before we got out of the state!

8 sheets nori (see seaweed, p. 8 and Helpful Hint below right)
4 cups warm cooked rice

Suggested filling combinations:
Avocado strips
Cucumber strips
Red bell pepper strips

Cabbage kimchi strips
Tofu strips
Steamed celery strips

Red bell pepper strips
Cucumber strips
Tofu strips

Pickled Korean or daikon radish strips (see glossary, p. 6)
Tofu strips
Green bell pepper strips

Sesame Spinach (p. 79)
Steamed carrot strips
Steamed Egg Strips (p. 164-65)

Steamed mushroom slices
Steamed carrot strips
Green bell pepper strips

1 teaspoon sesame salt (optional)

Condiments:
Hot Korean mustard (or mix 2 tablespoons dry mustard with 2 table-
    spoons water)
Pickled ginger
Soy sauce

1. Place a sheet of nori on a cutting board with the long side facing you. Spread ½ cup of rice over the bottom third of the sheet.

2. In a long line on top of the rice, place one of the filling combinations so that it extends across the width of the nori. Once the filling has been placed across the rice, gently press it into the rice. Sprinkle the rice and filling with a little sesame salt, if preferred.

3. Starting at the filling edge, roll the nori away from you, forming a cylindrical shape. Keep the nori roll snug and tight. When you have rolled to the end of the sheet, you may have to dampen the edge with water to seal it well. Repeat until all 8 nori sheets have been filled and rolled.

4. Place each seaweed roll on a cutting board. With a sharp knife, cut the roll crosswise into 8 or 9 pieces. Place on a platter, and serve with Korean mustard, pickled ginger, and/or soy sauce.

Helpful hint: Nori can be purchased in most well-stocked grocery stores.

Per serving: Calories: 236, Protein: 6 g, Fat: 4 g, Carbohydrates: 41 g

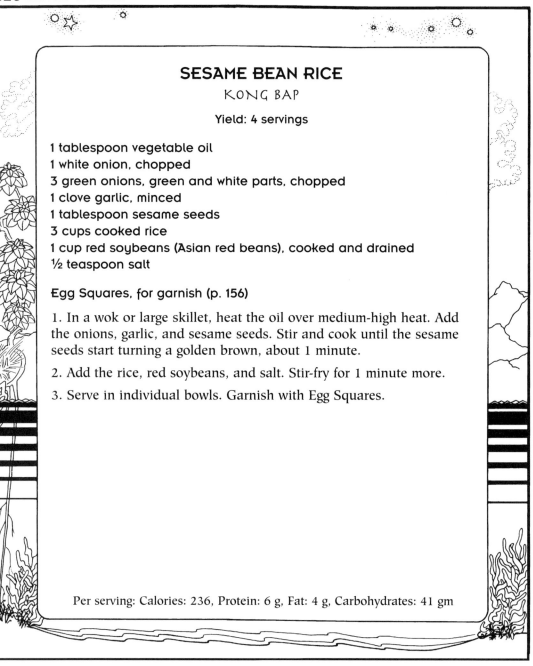

SESAME BEAN RICE
KONG BAP

Yield: 4 servings

1 tablespoon vegetable oil
1 white onion, chopped
3 green onions, green and white parts, chopped
1 clove garlic, minced
1 tablespoon sesame seeds
3 cups cooked rice
1 cup red soybeans (Asian red beans), cooked and drained
½ teaspoon salt

Egg Squares, for garnish (p. 156)

1. In a wok or large skillet, heat the oil over medium-high heat. Add the onions, garlic, and sesame seeds. Stir and cook until the sesame seeds start turning a golden brown, about 1 minute.

2. Add the rice, red soybeans, and salt. Stir-fry for 1 minute more.

3. Serve in individual bowls. Garnish with Egg Squares.

Per serving: Calories: 236, Protein: 6 g, Fat: 4 g, Carbohydrates: 41 gm

STICKY RICE

JEEN BAP

Yield: 3 cups (4 servings)

2 cups water
1 cup uncooked medium-grain white rice
1 tablespoon rice vinegar
½ tablespoon sugar
½ teaspoon salt

1. In a medium pan, bring the water to a boil. Add the rice and cover. Reduce the heat to low, and simmer for 15 minutes.

2. Remove from the heat and let stand 5 minutes. Transfer the rice to a large nonmetal bowl.

3. In a cup or small bowl, mix the rice vinegar, sugar, and salt. Pour over the rice and gently fold to combine. Serve warm or at room temperature.

Per cup: Calories: 166, Protein: 3 g, Fat: 0 g, Carbohydrates: 37 g

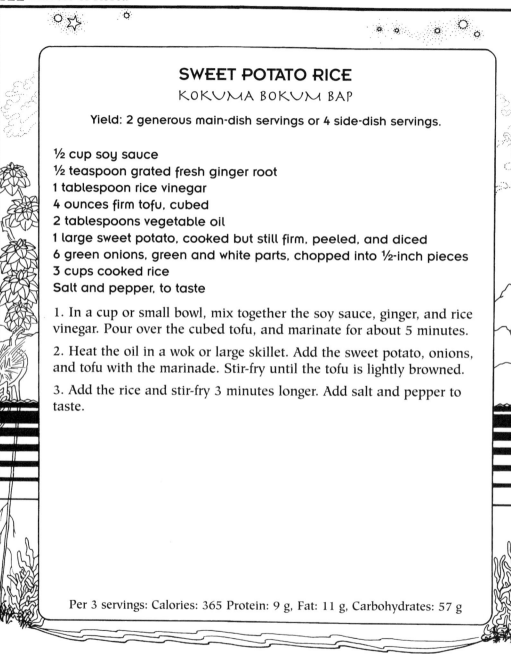

SWEET POTATO RICE
KOKUMA BOKUM BAP

Yield: 2 generous main-dish servings or 4 side-dish servings.

½ cup soy sauce
½ teaspoon grated fresh ginger root
1 tablespoon rice vinegar
4 ounces firm tofu, cubed
2 tablespoons vegetable oil
1 large sweet potato, cooked but still firm, peeled, and diced
6 green onions, green and white parts, chopped into ½-inch pieces
3 cups cooked rice
Salt and pepper, to taste

1. In a cup or small bowl, mix together the soy sauce, ginger, and rice vinegar. Pour over the cubed tofu, and marinate for about 5 minutes.

2. Heat the oil in a wok or large skillet. Add the sweet potato, onions, and tofu with the marinade. Stir-fry until the tofu is lightly browned.

3. Add the rice and stir-fry 3 minutes longer. Add salt and pepper to taste.

Per 3 servings: Calories: 365 Protein: 9 g, Fat: 11 g, Carbohydrates: 57 g

Noodles, Dumplings & Eggrolls

KUKSU E MANDU

If only all noodle dishes tasted as exciting as some of these Korean noodle dishes! Young's and my favorite recipe, Cucumber Noodles, is listed in this section. When I first tasted this unusual combination of hot pepper, cool cucumber, garlic, and onion, I was hooked on Korean cooking. The flavors were wonderful, the food was low-fat, and the preparation was quick and easy. What more could a cook ask for?

Although Cucumber Noodles is our favorite dish, there are numerous other unusual recipes in this section. Whether trying buckwheat noodles, sweet potato noodles, plump dumplings, or spicy eggrolls, unconventional flavor prevails. Korean cooks just seem to have a knack for dressing up bland foods with such fire and zest that the foods take on a whole new personality. And the recipes in this section certainly reflect that talent.

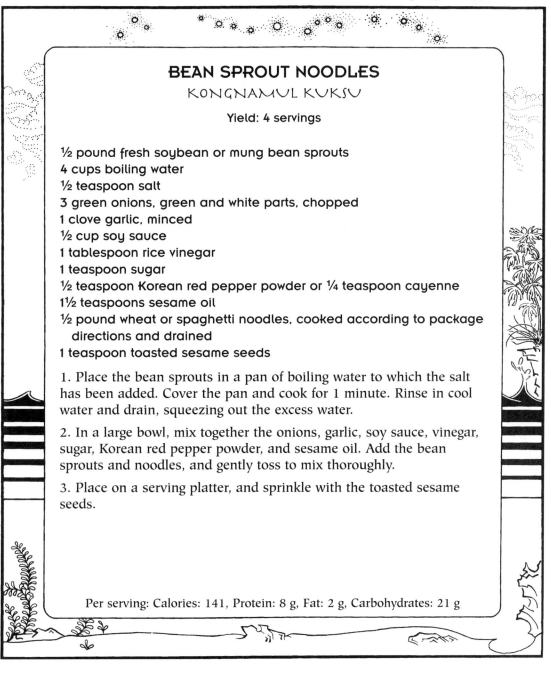

BEAN SPROUT NOODLES
KONGNAMUL KUKSU

Yield: 4 servings

½ pound fresh soybean or mung bean sprouts
4 cups boiling water
½ teaspoon salt
3 green onions, green and white parts, chopped
1 clove garlic, minced
½ cup soy sauce
1 tablespoon rice vinegar
1 teaspoon sugar
½ teaspoon Korean red pepper powder or ¼ teaspoon cayenne
1½ teaspoons sesame oil
½ pound wheat or spaghetti noodles, cooked according to package
   directions and drained
1 teaspoon toasted sesame seeds

1. Place the bean sprouts in a pan of boiling water to which the salt has been added. Cover the pan and cook for 1 minute. Rinse in cool water and drain, squeezing out the excess water.

2. In a large bowl, mix together the onions, garlic, soy sauce, vinegar, sugar, Korean red pepper powder, and sesame oil. Add the bean sprouts and noodles, and gently toss to mix thoroughly.

3. Place on a serving platter, and sprinkle with the toasted sesame seeds.

Per serving: Calories: 141, Protein: 8 g, Fat: 2 g, Carbohydrates: 21 g

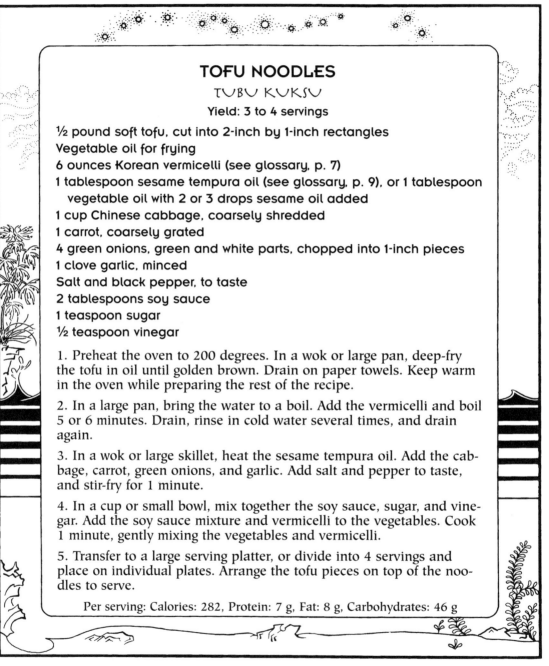

TOFU NOODLES

TUBU KUKSU

Yield: 3 to 4 servings

½ pound soft tofu, cut into 2-inch by 1-inch rectangles
Vegetable oil for frying
6 ounces Korean vermicelli (see glossary, p. 7)
1 tablespoon sesame tempura oil (see glossary, p. 9), or 1 tablespoon
  vegetable oil with 2 or 3 drops sesame oil added
1 cup Chinese cabbage, coarsely shredded
1 carrot, coarsely grated
4 green onions, green and white parts, chopped into 1-inch pieces
1 clove garlic, minced
Salt and black pepper, to taste
2 tablespoons soy sauce
1 teaspoon sugar
½ teaspoon vinegar

1. Preheat the oven to 200 degrees. In a wok or large pan, deep-fry
the tofu in oil until golden brown. Drain on paper towels. Keep warm
in the oven while preparing the rest of the recipe.

2. In a large pan, bring the water to a boil. Add the vermicelli and boil
5 or 6 minutes. Drain, rinse in cold water several times, and drain
again.

3. In a wok or large skillet, heat the sesame tempura oil. Add the cabbage, carrot, green onions, and garlic. Add salt and pepper to taste,
and stir-fry for 1 minute.

4. In a cup or small bowl, mix together the soy sauce, sugar, and vinegar. Add the soy sauce mixture and vermicelli to the vegetables. Cook
1 minute, gently mixing the vegetables and vermicelli.

5. Transfer to a large serving platter, or divide into 4 servings and
place on individual plates. Arrange the tofu pieces on top of the noodles to serve.

Per serving: Calories: 282, Protein: 7 g, Fat: 8 g, Carbohydrates: 46 g

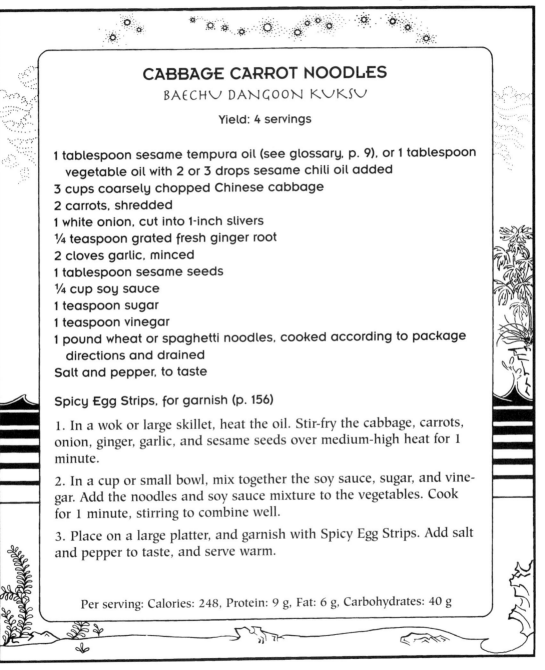

CABBAGE CARROT NOODLES
BAECHU DANGOON KUKSU

Yield: 4 servings

1 tablespoon sesame tempura oil (see glossary, p. 9), or 1 tablespoon
  vegetable oil with 2 or 3 drops sesame chili oil added
3 cups coarsely chopped Chinese cabbage
2 carrots, shredded
1 white onion, cut into 1-inch slivers
¼ teaspoon grated fresh ginger root
2 cloves garlic, minced
1 tablespoon sesame seeds
¼ cup soy sauce
1 teaspoon sugar
1 teaspoon vinegar
1 pound wheat or spaghetti noodles, cooked according to package
  directions and drained
Salt and pepper, to taste

Spicy Egg Strips, for garnish (p. 156)

1. In a wok or large skillet, heat the oil. Stir-fry the cabbage, carrots,
onion, ginger, garlic, and sesame seeds over medium-high heat for 1
minute.

2. In a cup or small bowl, mix together the soy sauce, sugar, and vinegar. Add the noodles and soy sauce mixture to the vegetables. Cook
for 1 minute, stirring to combine well.

3. Place on a large platter, and garnish with Spicy Egg Strips. Add salt
and pepper to taste, and serve warm.

Per serving: Calories: 248, Protein: 9 g, Fat: 6 g, Carbohydrates: 40 g

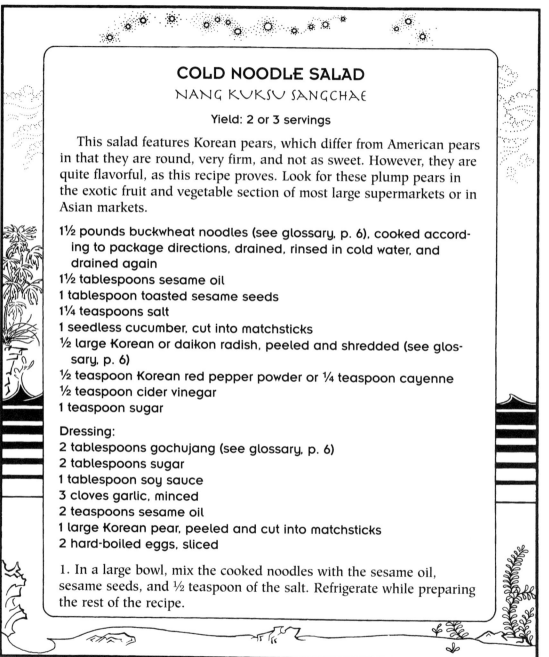

COLD NOODLE SALAD
NANG KUKSU SANGCHAE
Yield: 2 or 3 servings

This salad features Korean pears, which differ from American pears in that they are round, very firm, and not as sweet. However, they are quite flavorful, as this recipe proves. Look for these plump pears in the exotic fruit and vegetable section of most large supermarkets or in Asian markets.

1½ pounds buckwheat noodles (see glossary, p. 6), cooked according to package directions, drained, rinsed in cold water, and drained again
1½ tablespoons sesame oil
1 tablespoon toasted sesame seeds
1¼ teaspoons salt
1 seedless cucumber, cut into matchsticks
½ large Korean or daikon radish, peeled and shredded (see glossary, p. 6)
½ teaspoon Korean red pepper powder or ¼ teaspoon cayenne
½ teaspoon cider vinegar
1 teaspoon sugar

Dressing:
2 tablespoons gochujang (see glossary, p. 6)
2 tablespoons sugar
1 tablespoon soy sauce
3 cloves garlic, minced
2 teaspoons sesame oil
1 large Korean pear, peeled and cut into matchsticks
2 hard-boiled eggs, sliced

1. In a large bowl, mix the cooked noodles with the sesame oil, sesame seeds, and ½ teaspoon of the salt. Refrigerate while preparing the rest of the recipe.

2. Sprinkle the cucumber strips with ¼ teaspoon of the salt, and let stand for 10 minutes. Pat dry with paper towels.

3. Sprinkle the shredded radish with the remaining ½ teaspoon salt, and let stand for 10 minutes. Squeeze out the liquid. In a bowl, mix together the radish, Korean red pepper powder, vinegar, and sugar.

4. Mix together the dressing ingredients in a cup or small bowl.

5. Place the noodles in a large bowl or serving platter. Arrange the vegetables and Korean pear in separate groups on top of the noodles. The egg slices can be decoratively placed in the middle of the salad in a flower pattern. Serve this dish cold or at room temperature with individual diners helping themselves to the dressing.

Per serving: Calories: 1213, Protein: 31 g, Fat: 18 g, Carbohydrates: 232 g

CUCUMBER NOODLES
OI KUKSU MUCHIM

Yield: 4 generous servings or 6 medium servings

This recipe was the inspiration for this cookbook and is the Korean dish most often requested by our families and friends. It presents a delicious balance between hot pepper and cool cucumber.

1 pound wheat noodles or spaghetti
½ cup soy sauce
¼ cup rice vinegar
1 tablespoon sugar
2 teaspoons sesame oil
2 tablespoons gochujang (see glossary, p. 6)
2 cloves garlic, minced
6 green onions, green and white parts, minced
1 large seedless cucumber, peeled and cut into matchsticks (Reserve some of the longer cucumber peels for garnish.)
2 hardboiled eggs, sliced

1. Boil the noodles according to package directions. After the noodles are cooked, drain and rinse them in cold water. Transfer to a large bowl.

2. In a small bowl, thoroughly mix together the soy sauce, vinegar, sugar, sesame oil, and gochujang. Add the garlic, onions, and cucumber.

3. Add the soy sauce mixture to the noodles, and toss gently to mix thoroughly.

4. Mound on a large platter, and arrange the egg slices in a flower pattern. Use the reserved cucumber peels as leaves and stems for the floral design.

Per 5 servings: Calories: 194, Protein: 10 g, Fat: 4 g, Carbohydrates: 28 g

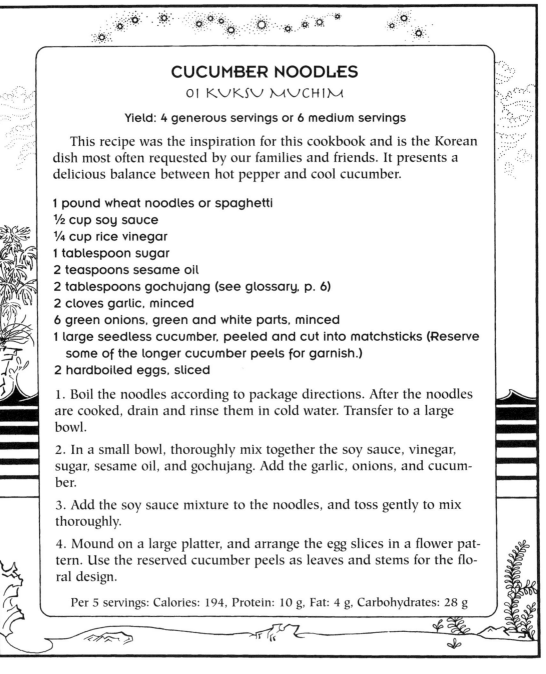

EGG NOODLES
KALJAEBI

Yield: 2 servings

1 cup all-purpose white flour
1 large egg
½ teaspoon salt
1 tablespoon water

1. On a large board, pile the flour into a mound with a well in the center. Drop in the egg and salt. Add the water and beat with a fork.

2. With your hands, add the flour from the outer edges of the mound to the wet ingredients a little at a time, and mix well. When the flour and wet ingredients are combined, knead the dough until smooth and no longer sticky.

3. Sprinkle some flour on a large, flat surface. With a rolling pin, roll the dough into a very thin sheet. Let dry about 10 minutes.

4. Sprinkle the dough lightly with flour. Tightly roll up the dough into a cylinder. With a sharp knife, slice the cylinder crosswise into thin strips. Unroll the noodles and allow to dry for 2 hours.

5. To cook, boil in salted water until the noodles rise to the water surface, about 10 minutes. Drain, rinse in cool water, and drain again.

6. The noodles can be used in any noodle recipe or simply served with soy sauce and a little sesame oil.

Per serving: Calories: 240, Protein: 9 g, Fat: 3 g, Carbohydrates: 43 g

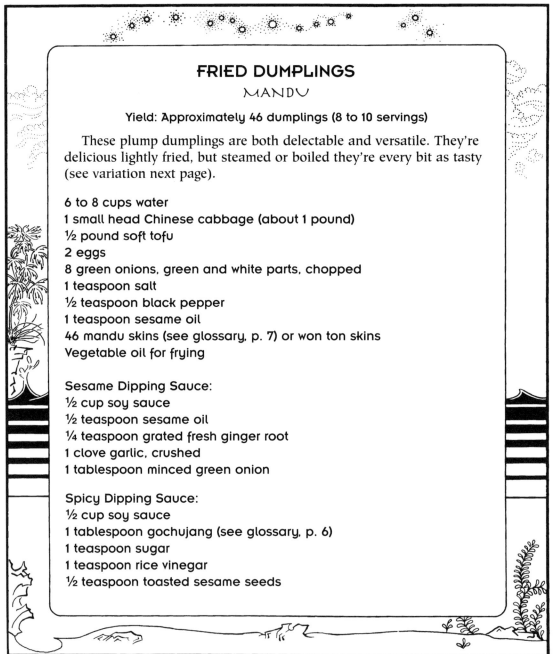

FRIED DUMPLINGS
MANDU

Yield: Approximately 46 dumplings (8 to 10 servings)

These plump dumplings are both delectable and versatile. They're delicious lightly fried, but steamed or boiled they're every bit as tasty (see variation next page).

6 to 8 cups water
1 small head Chinese cabbage (about 1 pound)
½ pound soft tofu
2 eggs
8 green onions, green and white parts, chopped
1 teaspoon salt
½ teaspoon black pepper
1 teaspoon sesame oil
46 mandu skins (see glossary, p. 7) or won ton skins
Vegetable oil for frying

Sesame Dipping Sauce:
½ cup soy sauce
½ teaspoon sesame oil
¼ teaspoon grated fresh ginger root
1 clove garlic, crushed
1 tablespoon minced green onion

Spicy Dipping Sauce:
½ cup soy sauce
1 tablespoon gochujang (see glossary, p. 6)
1 teaspoon sugar
1 teaspoon rice vinegar
½ teaspoon toasted sesame seeds

1. In a large pan, bring the water to a boil. Parboil the Chinese cabbage for 5 minutes, then drain thoroughly. Blot the cabbage with a towel to dry it completely, and cut off the thick, white end. Finely chop or shred the cabbage, and place in a large bowl.

2. Drain the tofu and squeeze out any excess water. Mash with a fork and add to the cabbage. Beat 1 egg. Add to the cabbage mixture, and stir to mix. Add the onions, salt, pepper, and sesame oil. Mix thoroughly. Beat the remaining egg and set aside. This will be used to seal the mandu or won ton skins.

3. Lay a mandu or won ton skin on a flat surface. Moisten the bottom edge of the mandu skin with some beaten egg. Place 1 teaspoon of the cabbage mixture just below center on the bottom half of the skin. Fold the top half of the skin over the filling to form a half-moon shape, and press the edges together to form a tight seal. Continue until all the filling and/or skins have been used.

4. In a large skillet, heat 1 tablespoon of the vegetable oil. Over moderate heat, cook 9 or 10 dumplings flat-side down. Fry until the bottoms are golden brown, about 1 minute. Turn the dumplings over. Add just enough water to cover the bottom of the pan. Cover the pan and steam until the water has evaporated, about 3 to 4 minutes. Remove the dumplings from the pan, and repeat for the remaining dumplings.

5. To make the dipping sauces, mix the ingredients together in separate small bowls. Serve with the dumplings.

Variation: These dumplings also can be steamed or boiled. If using a steamer, steam for about 20 minutes. To boil the dumplings, season

the boiling water with 1 clove garlic, chopped, ½ teaspoon salt, and ½ teaspoon sesame oil. Boil gently until the dumplings float to the top of the water and appear transparent, about 10 minutes.

Per dumpling without sauce:

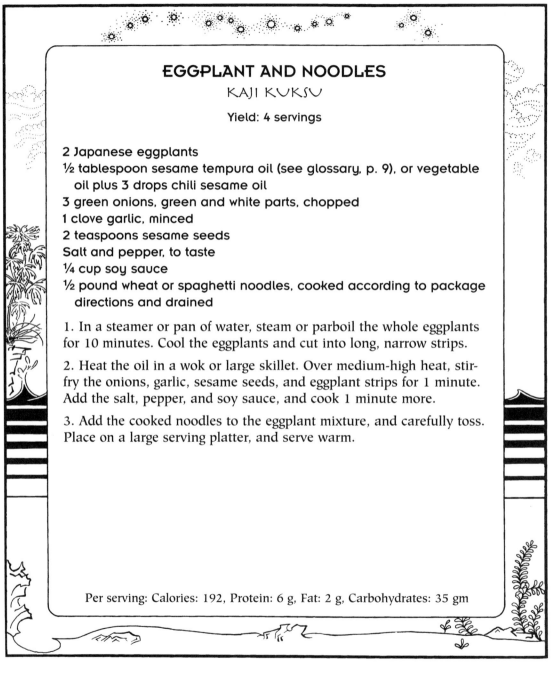

EGGPLANT AND NOODLES
KAJI KUKSU

Yield: 4 servings

2 Japanese eggplants
½ tablespoon sesame tempura oil (see glossary, p. 9), or vegetable
  oil plus 3 drops chili sesame oil
3 green onions, green and white parts, chopped
1 clove garlic, minced
2 teaspoons sesame seeds
Salt and pepper, to taste
¼ cup soy sauce
½ pound wheat or spaghetti noodles, cooked according to package
  directions and drained

1. In a steamer or pan of water, steam or parboil the whole eggplants
for 10 minutes. Cool the eggplants and cut into long, narrow strips.

2. Heat the oil in a wok or large skillet. Over medium-high heat, stir-
fry the onions, garlic, sesame seeds, and eggplant strips for 1 minute.
Add the salt, pepper, and soy sauce, and cook 1 minute more.

3. Add the cooked noodles to the eggplant mixture, and carefully toss.
Place on a large serving platter, and serve warm.

Per serving: Calories: 192, Protein: 6 g, Fat: 2 g, Carbohydrates: 35 gm

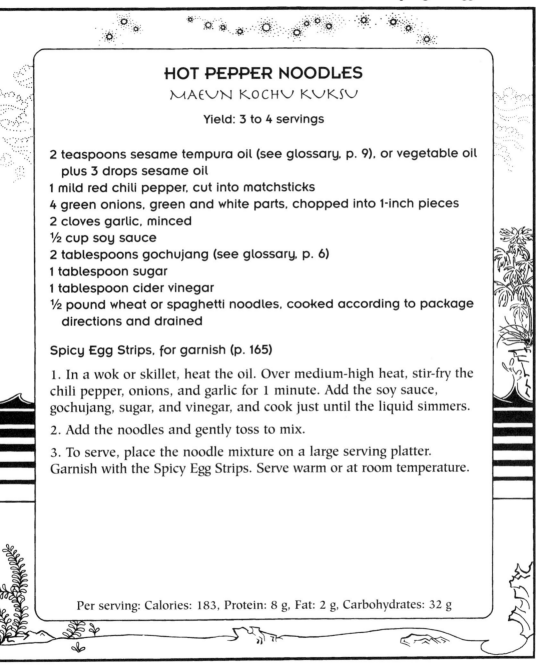

HOT PEPPER NOODLES

MAEUN KOCHU KUKSU

Yield: 3 to 4 servings

2 teaspoons sesame tempura oil (see glossary, p. 9), or vegetable oil
plus 3 drops sesame oil
1 mild red chili pepper, cut into matchsticks
4 green onions, green and white parts, chopped into 1-inch pieces
2 cloves garlic, minced
½ cup soy sauce
2 tablespoons gochujang (see glossary, p. 6)
1 tablespoon sugar
1 tablespoon cider vinegar
½ pound wheat or spaghetti noodles, cooked according to package
directions and drained

Spicy Egg Strips, for garnish (p. 165)

1. In a wok or skillet, heat the oil. Over medium-high heat, stir-fry the
chili pepper, onions, and garlic for 1 minute. Add the soy sauce,
gochujang, sugar, and vinegar, and cook just until the liquid simmers.

2. Add the noodles and gently toss to mix.

3. To serve, place the noodle mixture on a large serving platter.
Garnish with the Spicy Egg Strips. Serve warm or at room temperature.

Per serving: Calories: 183, Protein: 8 g, Fat: 2 g, Carbohydrates: 32 g

FRIED KIMCHI EGGROLLS
KIMCHI MANDU

Yield: Approximately 18 eggrolls (9 servings)

These eggrolls are a cross between Korean and Chinese—spicy Korean fillings and crispy Chinese eggroll wrappers. An unusual but tasty creation.

2 teaspoons sesame tempura oil (see glossary, p. 9), or vegetable oil
    plus 4 drops sesame oil
½ cup chopped fresh button mushrooms
3 green onions, green and white parts, minced
2 cloves garlic, minced
1 teaspoon sesame seeds
2 cups cabbage kimchi, minced (p. 36)
½ pound fresh soybean or mung bean sprouts, parboiled, drained,
    and squeezed dry
¼ teaspoon salt, or more to taste
¼ teaspoon black pepper
2 hard-boiled eggs, chopped
1 egg, beaten
18 eggroll skins
Vegetable oil for frying

1. In a skillet, heat the sesame oil. Over medium-high heat, sauté the mushrooms, green onions, garlic, and sesame seeds for 1 minute. Transfer to a large bowl.

2. Add the kimchi, bean sprouts, salt, pepper, and eggs to the mushroom mixture, and mix well.

3. Place an eggroll skin on a flat surface. Place 1 heaping tablespoon of kimchi mixture on the eggroll skin. Fold 1 side of the eggroll skin over the filling. Then fold the 2 side points of the eggroll skin over the

filling. Moisten the unrolled edge of the eggroll skin with the beaten egg. Roll the eggroll closed, ensuring that the edge seals tightly. Repeat until all the filling and/or eggroll skins have been used.

4. In a deep pan or wok, heat the oil for deep frying. Place no more than 2 or 3 eggrolls in the pan at a time to prevent the oil from boiling over. Deep-fry until golden brown, about 3 minutes. Remove from the pan and drain on paper towels.

5. Serve warm with Korean mustard and soy sauce.

Per eggroll: Calories: 44, Protein: 2 g, Fat: 1 g, Carbohydrates: 5 g

MUSHROOM NOODLES

BOSOT KUKSU

Yield: 4 servings

½ tablespoon sesame tempura oil (see glossary, p. 9), or vegetable oil plus 3 drops sesame oil
½ pound fresh button mushrooms, sliced
1 mild red chili pepper, cut into matchsticks
2 cloves garlic, minced
¼ cup soy sauce
¼ cup white wine
1 pound wheat noodles or spaghetti, cooked according to package directions and drained
1 green onion, green and white parts, minced

1. In a wok or large skillet, heat the oil over medium-high heat. Add the mushrooms, chili pepper, and garlic. Stir-fry for 1 minute.

2. Add the wine and soy sauce, and cook for 1 minute.

3. Add the noodles and gently mix. Transfer to a large serving platter, and garnish with the onion before serving.

Per serving: Calories: 209, Protein: 9 g, Fat: 2 g, Carbohydrates: 34 g

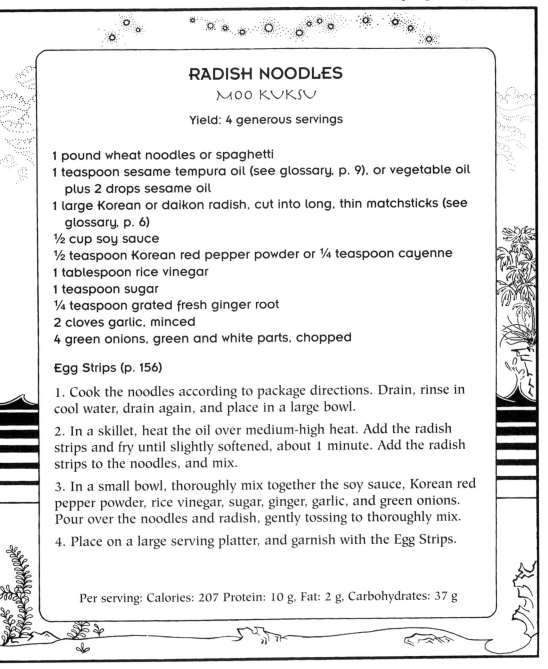

RADISH NOODLES
MOO KUKSU

Yield: 4 generous servings

1 pound wheat noodles or spaghetti
1 teaspoon sesame tempura oil (see glossary, p. 9), or vegetable oil
  plus 2 drops sesame oil
1 large Korean or daikon radish, cut into long, thin matchsticks (see
  glossary, p. 6)
½ cup soy sauce
½ teaspoon Korean red pepper powder or ¼ teaspoon cayenne
1 tablespoon rice vinegar
1 teaspoon sugar
¼ teaspoon grated fresh ginger root
2 cloves garlic, minced
4 green onions, green and white parts, chopped

Egg Strips (p. 156)

1. Cook the noodles according to package directions. Drain, rinse in cool water, drain again, and place in a large bowl.

2. In a skillet, heat the oil over medium-high heat. Add the radish strips and fry until slightly softened, about 1 minute. Add the radish strips to the noodles, and mix.

3. In a small bowl, thoroughly mix together the soy sauce, Korean red pepper powder, rice vinegar, sugar, ginger, garlic, and green onions. Pour over the noodles and radish, gently tossing to thoroughly mix.

4. Place on a large serving platter, and garnish with the Egg Strips.

Per serving: Calories: 207 Protein: 10 g, Fat: 2 g, Carbohydrates: 37 g

SESAME NOODLES

BIBIM KUKSU

Yield: 4 servings

1 teaspoon vegetable oil
2 tablespoons sesame seeds
½ cup soy sauce
1 tablespoon rice vinegar
1 teaspoon sugar
1½ teaspoons sesame oil
1 clove garlic, crushed
¼ teaspoon grated fresh ginger root
¼ pound wheat noodles, cooked according to package directions
    and drained

2 hard-boiled eggs, sliced, or Spicy Egg Strips (p. 165)

1. In a small skillet, heat the oil over medium-high heat. Add the sesame seeds. Stirring constantly, cook the sesame seeds until light golden brown, about 1 minute.

2. In a small bowl, mix together the soy sauce, rice vinegar, sugar, sesame oil, garlic, and ginger.

3. Place the noodles in a large bowl. Add the toasted sesame seeds and the soy sauce mixture. Toss gently to coat. Transfer to a large platter, and garnish with the egg slices or Spicy Egg Strips. Serve warm or at room temperature.

Per serving: Calories: 184, Protein: 9 g, Fat: 9 g, Carbohydrates: 19 g

STEAMED KIMCHI DUMPLINGS

KIMCHI CHIN MANDU

Yield: Approximately 46 dumplings (6 to 8 servings)

There's no sublety about the taste of this spicy dumpling. The kimchi filling imparts just enough bite to let you know it's there.

2 cups cabbage kimchi (p. 36), drained, liquid reserved, and minced
½ pound fresh tofu, squeezed and crumbled
1 egg, beaten
½ teaspoon salt
¼ teaspoon pepper
46 round mandu or won ton skins
1 egg, beaten
2 green onions, green and white parts, minced

1. Mix together the chopped kimchi, crumbled tofu, 1 egg, salt, and pepper.

2. Lay a mandu skin on a flat surface. Moisten the bottom edge of the mandu skin with some of the single beaten egg. Place heaping 1 teaspoon of the kimchi mixture just below the center on the bottom half of the skin. Fold the top half of the skin over the filling to form a half-moon shape, and press the edges together to form a tight seal. Continue until all the filling and/or skins have been used.

3. Steam the dumplings in a steamer for at least 20 minutes.

4. To serve, heat the reserved kimchi liquid, and drizzle over the dumplings. Garnish with the green onions, and serve warm.

Per dumpling: Calories: 33 Protein: 2 g, Fat: 0 g, Carbohydrates: 5 g

DEB'S VEGETABLE NOODLES

JAP CHAE

Yield: 4 servings.

Jap chae is a mix-and-match medley of sweet potato noodles and various vegetables lightly seasoned with sugar, sesame, and soy sauce. Young and I have provided two of our favorite versions of this popular Korean dish, but you may substitute ingredients to suite your own taste.

My version calls for sesame chili oil, which makes for a spicier dish, and the addition of tree ears, mushrooms which are frequently used in classic jap chae. Tree ears are also called cloud ears or black fungus and can be purchased dried in small packages in Asian markets or well-stocked grocery stores. Simply reconstitute them in warm water for about ½ hour before using.

6 cups water
6 ounces Korean vermicelli (see glossary, p. 7)
1 tablespoon vegetable oil
1 red bell pepper, cut into matchsticks
½ white onion, cut into strips
2 green onions, green and white parts, chopped into 1-inch pieces
1 seedless cucumber or 1 small zucchini, cut into matchsticks
2 cloves garlic, minced
¼ cup tree ears, soaked in warm water for ½ hour, then thoroughly
    drained
2 cups fresh soybean or mung bean sprouts, parboiled, drained,
    and squeezed
¼ teaspoon salt
¼ teaspoon pepper
½ tablespoon sesame chili oil (see glossary, p. 9)
3 tablespoons soy sauce

1 tablespoon sugar
½ tablespoon rice vinegar
2 teaspoons sesame seeds

Egg Strips, for garnish (p. 156)

1. In a large pan, bring the water to a boil. Add the vermicelli and cook until al dente, about 6 to 7 minutes. Drain, rinse several times in cold water, and drain again. Set aside.

2. In a wok or skillet, heat the oil. Over medium-high heat, stir-fry the red pepper, onions, cucumber or zucchini, garlic, and tree ears for 1 minute. Add the bean sprouts, salt, and pepper, and cook 1 minute more. Remove from the heat and set aside. Transfer to a bowl.

3. In the same wok or skillet, heat the sesame chili oil. Over medium heat, fry the vermicelli, soy sauce, sugar, vinegar, and sesame seeds for 1 minute. Add the mushroom mixture and gently mix the noodles and vegetables together.

4. Transfer to a large serving platter or individual plates. Garnish with Egg Strips. Serve warm or at room temperature.

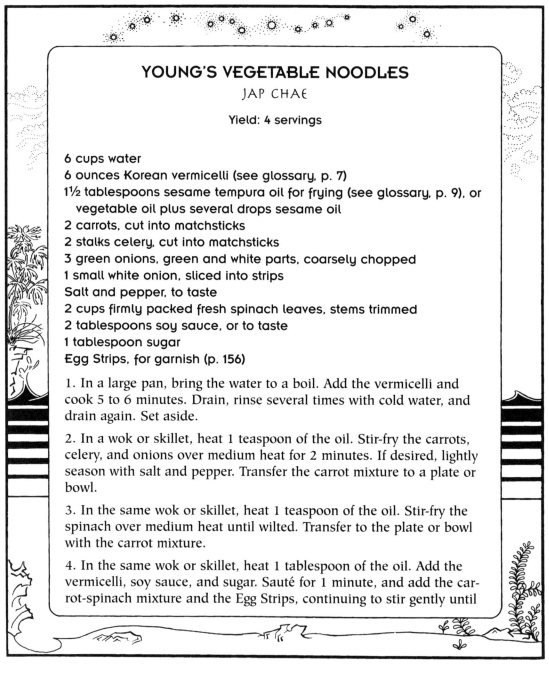

YOUNG'S VEGETABLE NOODLES

JAP CHAE

Yield: 4 servings

6 cups water
6 ounces Korean vermicelli (see glossary, p. 7)
1½ tablespoons sesame tempura oil for frying (see glossary, p. 9), or
    vegetable oil plus several drops sesame oil
2 carrots, cut into matchsticks
2 stalks celery, cut into matchsticks
3 green onions, green and white parts, coarsely chopped
1 small white onion, sliced into strips
Salt and pepper, to taste
2 cups firmly packed fresh spinach leaves, stems trimmed
2 tablespoons soy sauce, or to taste
1 tablespoon sugar
Egg Strips, for garnish (p. 156)

1. In a large pan, bring the water to a boil. Add the vermicelli and cook 5 to 6 minutes. Drain, rinse several times with cold water, and drain again. Set aside.

2. In a wok or skillet, heat 1 teaspoon of the oil. Stir-fry the carrots, celery, and onions over medium heat for 2 minutes. If desired, lightly season with salt and pepper. Transfer the carrot mixture to a plate or bowl.

3. In the same wok or skillet, heat 1 teaspoon of the oil. Stir-fry the spinach over medium heat until wilted. Transfer to the plate or bowl with the carrot mixture.

4. In the same wok or skillet, heat 1 tablespoon of the oil. Add the vermicelli, soy sauce, and sugar. Sauté for 1 minute, and add the carrot-spinach mixture and the Egg Strips, continuing to stir gently until

the vegetables and egg are thoroughly mixed in with the vermicelli. Season with salt and pepper to taste.

5. Serve warm or cold on a large platter or in individual bowls.

Per serving: Calories: 247, Protein: 3 g, Fat: 6 g, Carbohydrates: 45 g

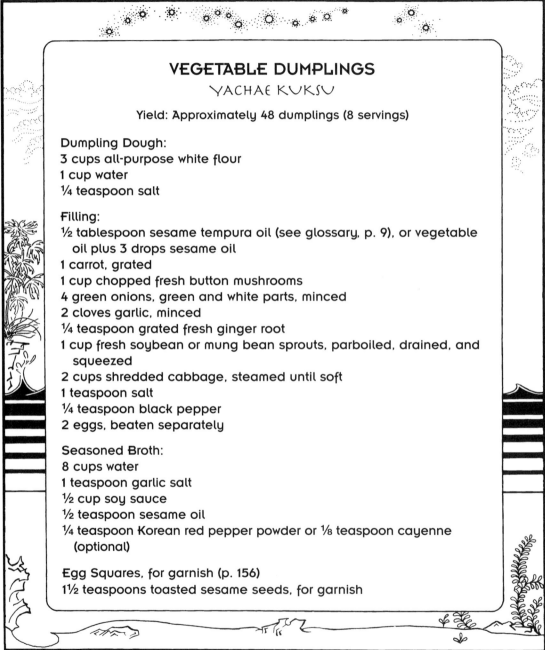

VEGETABLE DUMPLINGS
YACHAE KUKSU

Yield: Approximately 48 dumplings (8 servings)

Dumpling Dough:
3 cups all-purpose white flour
1 cup water
¼ teaspoon salt

Filling:
½ tablespoon sesame tempura oil (see glossary, p. 9), or vegetable oil plus 3 drops sesame oil
1 carrot, grated
1 cup chopped fresh button mushrooms
4 green onions, green and white parts, minced
2 cloves garlic, minced
¼ teaspoon grated fresh ginger root
1 cup fresh soybean or mung bean sprouts, parboiled, drained, and squeezed
2 cups shredded cabbage, steamed until soft
1 teaspoon salt
¼ teaspoon black pepper
2 eggs, beaten separately

Seasoned Broth:
8 cups water
1 teaspoon garlic salt
½ cup soy sauce
½ teaspoon sesame oil
¼ teaspoon Korean red pepper powder or ⅛ teaspoon cayenne (optional)

Egg Squares, for garnish (p. 156)
1½ teaspoons toasted sesame seeds, for garnish

1. To make the dumpling dough, mix together the flour, water, and salt in a bowl. Knead until the dough is smooth and elastic, about 5 to 10 minutes. Let the dough rest for 30 minutes. Divide the dough in half, and roll each half into a very thin sheet, about 1/16 inch thick. Lightly sprinkle the dough and/or rolling pin with flour to keep the dough from sticking. Using a 3-inch round cookie or biscuit cutter, cut out circles for each dumpling.

2. To make the filling, heat the oil in a wok or large skillet. Fry the carrot, mushrooms, onions, garlic, and ginger for 1 minute. Remove from the heat and set aside.

3. In a large bowl, mix together the sprouts, cabbage, salt, and pepper. Add the carrot mixture and 1 beaten egg. Stir to mix thoroughly. Transfer to a wire colander to keep the mixture drained as you assemble the dumplings.

4. Lay a circle of dough on a flat surface. Moisten the edges with a little beaten egg. Place ½ tablespoon of carrot mixture in the middle of each circle of dough. Fold the top of the circle over the filling, and press the edges together to form a tight seal. Press the edges of the dumplings up so that the dumpling is round instead of a half-moon shape. (Each dumpling should resemble a plump sailor's hat with upturned brim.) Repeat until all the filling and/or dough has been used.

5. Add the broth ingredients to a large pan, and bring to a boil over medium-high heat. Gently drop the dumplings into the boiling broth. They will rise to the surface as they cook. Cook until the dumpling skins look transparent, about 3 minutes.

6. To serve, place the dumplings in individual serving bowls, and cover with broth. Garnish with Egg Squares and the sesame seeds.

Note: Vegetable Dumplings can be prepared in advance and frozen for later use. Freeze them after assembling and before cooking.

Per serving: Calories: 204, Protein: 8 g, Fat: 3 g, Carbohydrates: 36 g

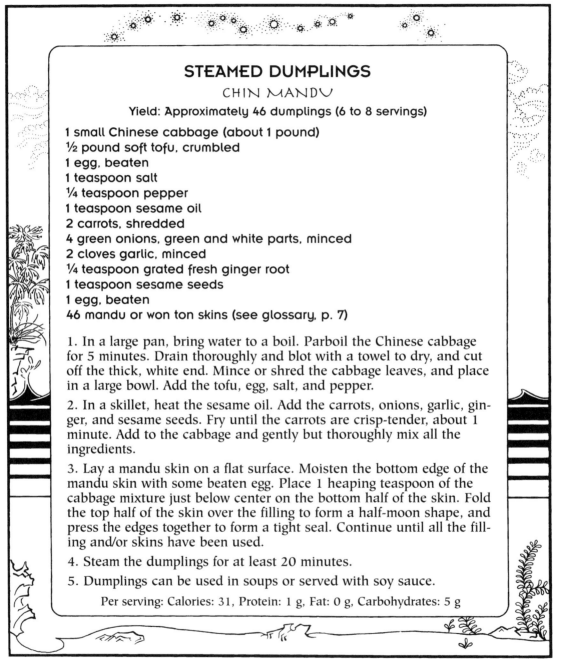

STEAMED DUMPLINGS

CHIN MANDU

Yield: Approximately 46 dumplings (6 to 8 servings)

1 small Chinese cabbage (about 1 pound)
½ pound soft tofu, crumbled
1 egg, beaten
1 teaspoon salt
¼ teaspoon pepper
1 teaspoon sesame oil
2 carrots, shredded
4 green onions, green and white parts, minced
2 cloves garlic, minced
¼ teaspoon grated fresh ginger root
1 teaspoon sesame seeds
1 egg, beaten
46 mandu or won ton skins (see glossary, p. 7)

1. In a large pan, bring water to a boil. Parboil the Chinese cabbage for 5 minutes. Drain thoroughly and blot with a towel to dry, and cut off the thick, white end. Mince or shred the cabbage leaves, and place in a large bowl. Add the tofu, egg, salt, and pepper.

2. In a skillet, heat the sesame oil. Add the carrots, onions, garlic, ginger, and sesame seeds. Fry until the carrots are crisp-tender, about 1 minute. Add to the cabbage and gently but thoroughly mix all the ingredients.

3. Lay a mandu skin on a flat surface. Moisten the bottom edge of the mandu skin with some beaten egg. Place 1 heaping teaspoon of the cabbage mixture just below center on the bottom half of the skin. Fold the top half of the skin over the filling to form a half-moon shape, and press the edges together to form a tight seal. Continue until all the filling and/or skins have been used.

4. Steam the dumplings for at least 20 minutes.

5. Dumplings can be used in soups or served with soy sauce.

Per serving: Calories: 31, Protein: 1 g, Fat: 0 g, Carbohydrates: 5 g

Tofu & Egg Dishes

TUBU E GERAN

This section covers tofu (or, as Koreans know it, tubu or bean curd) and eggs prepared the Korean way—protein with spirit. Even the nondescript flavor of tofu takes on personality with the blessing of Korean seasonings. Firm tofu is preferred by many Korean cooks, but soft tofu may be substituted in some of these recipes if so desired. If possible, try to purchase fresh tofu blocks available in Asian markets. These wonderful, creamy creations have a consummate superiority in texture and taste to the plastic-wrapped chunks found in most supermarkets.

Korean cooks generally view eggs as an accompaniment or adornment to a meal rather than as an entrée. Egg squares or strips are used as a garnish; hardboiled eggs are sliced and used as decoration. But to accommodate egg lovers, we have exercised creative license and included some main-dish egg recipes too. Enjoy.

BARBECUED TOFU
TUBU KUI

Yield: 4 servings

The marinade used in this recipe is a spicy concoction that will inject plenty of fire into the mild-flavored tofu.

Marinade:
½ cup soy sauce
¼ cup rice vinegar
1 tablespoon gochujang (see glossary, p. 6)
2 teaspoons sugar
2 cloves garlic, crushed

1 pound firm tofu, cut into slices 3 inches long by 1 inch wide by
    ½ inch thick
1½ tablespoons sesame tempura oil (see glossary, p. 9), or vegetable oil plus 2 or 3 drops sesame oil

1. Mix the marinade ingredients in a small saucepan. Bring to a boil, stirring to dissolve the gochujang and sugar. Remove from the heat.

2. Place the tofu slices in a large, plastic sealable bag or a small bowl. Pour the marinade over the tofu, coating all the slices. Place in the refrigerator and marinate for 8 hours or overnight. Drain; discard the marinade.

3. In a large skillet, heat the oil over medium-high heat. Place 4 tofu slices in the pan, and cook until lightly browned, about 3 minutes. Turn the tofu slices over, and brown the other sides. Transfer to a platter and repeat with the remaining tofu slices.

Variations: Tofu slices can also be grilled or broiled. Before grilling or broiling, lightly brush the tofu slices with sesame tempura oil.

Per serving: Calories: 176, Protein: 11 g, Fat: 9 g, Carbohydrates: 10 g

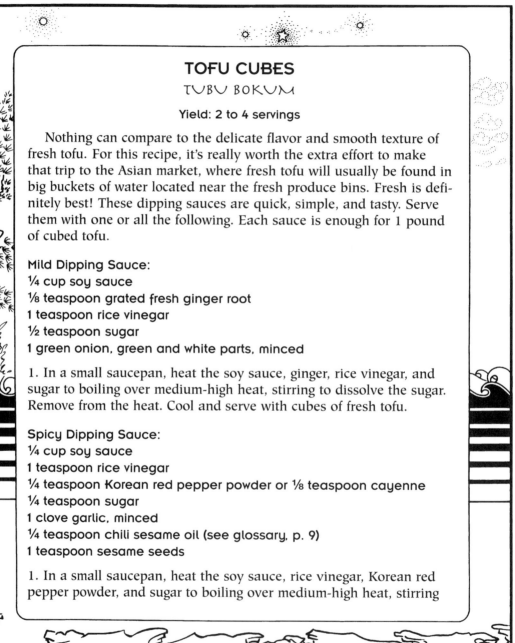

TOFU CUBES
TUBU BOKUM

Yield: 2 to 4 servings

Nothing can compare to the delicate flavor and smooth texture of fresh tofu. For this recipe, it's really worth the extra effort to make that trip to the Asian market, where fresh tofu will usually be found in big buckets of water located near the fresh produce bins. Fresh is definitely best! These dipping sauces are quick, simple, and tasty. Serve them with one or all the following. Each sauce is enough for 1 pound of cubed tofu.

Mild Dipping Sauce:
¼ cup soy sauce
⅛ teaspoon grated fresh ginger root
1 teaspoon rice vinegar
½ teaspoon sugar
1 green onion, green and white parts, minced

1. In a small saucepan, heat the soy sauce, ginger, rice vinegar, and sugar to boiling over medium-high heat, stirring to dissolve the sugar. Remove from the heat. Cool and serve with cubes of fresh tofu.

Spicy Dipping Sauce:
¼ cup soy sauce
1 teaspoon rice vinegar
¼ teaspoon Korean red pepper powder or ⅛ teaspoon cayenne
¼ teaspoon sugar
1 clove garlic, minced
¼ teaspoon chili sesame oil (see glossary, p. 9)
1 teaspoon sesame seeds

1. In a small saucepan, heat the soy sauce, rice vinegar, Korean red pepper powder, and sugar to boiling over medium-high heat, stirring

until the Korean red pepper powder and sugar are dissolved. Remove from the heat and add the garlic.

2. In a small nonstick skillet, heat the oil over medium-high heat. Add the sesame seeds. Stir and cook until the sesame seeds are lightly browned, about 1 minute. Mix the sesame seeds and soy sauce mixture together. Serve with cubes of fresh tofu.

Fiery Dipping Sauce:
¼ cup soy sauce
2 tablespoons gochujang (see glossary, p. 6)
1 teaspoon rice vinegar
½ teaspoon sugar
1 teaspoon minced green onion, green and white parts

1. In a small saucepan, heat the soy sauce, gochujang, rice vinegar, and sugar to boiling, stirring constantly until the gochujang and sugar are dissolved. Remove from the heat. Garnish with the minced onion.

2. Serve with cubes of fresh tofu.

Per serving: Calories: 133 Protein: 13 g, Fat: 6 g, Carbohydrates: 5 g

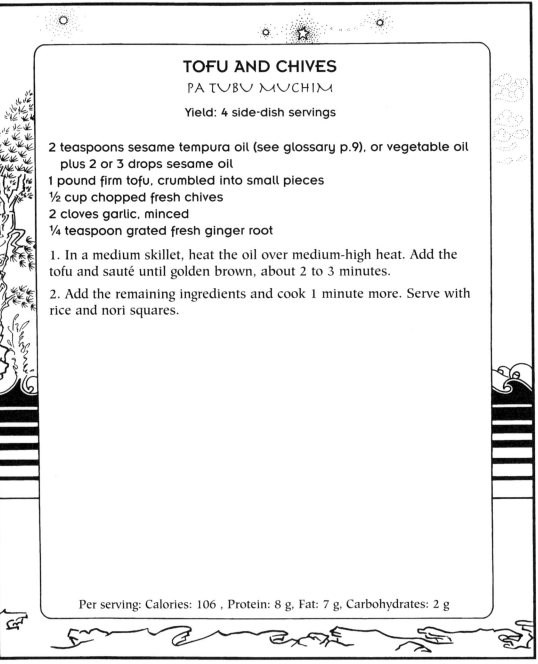

TOFU AND CHIVES

PA TUBU MUCHIM

Yield: 4 side-dish servings

2 teaspoons sesame tempura oil (see glossary p.9), or vegetable oil
    plus 2 or 3 drops sesame oil
1 pound firm tofu, crumbled into small pieces
½ cup chopped fresh chives
2 cloves garlic, minced
¼ teaspoon grated fresh ginger root

1. In a medium skillet, heat the oil over medium-high heat. Add the tofu and sauté until golden brown, about 2 to 3 minutes.

2. Add the remaining ingredients and cook 1 minute more. Serve with rice and nori squares.

Per serving: Calories: 106 , Protein: 8 g, Fat: 7 g, Carbohydrates: 2 g

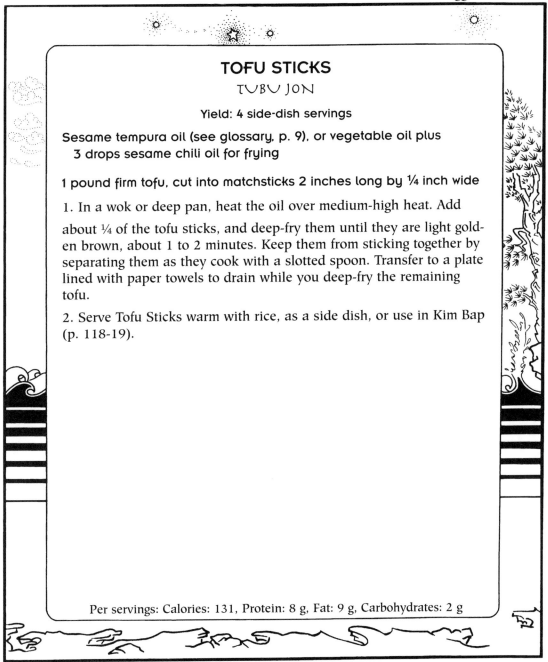

TOFU STICKS

TUBU JON

Yield: 4 side-dish servings

Sesame tempura oil (see glossary, p. 9), or vegetable oil plus
  3 drops sesame chili oil for frying

1 pound firm tofu, cut into matchsticks 2 inches long by ¼ inch wide

1. In a wok or deep pan, heat the oil over medium-high heat. Add about ¼ of the tofu sticks, and deep-fry them until they are light golden brown, about 1 to 2 minutes. Keep them from sticking together by separating them as they cook with a slotted spoon. Transfer to a plate lined with paper towels to drain while you deep-fry the remaining tofu.

2. Serve Tofu Sticks warm with rice, as a side dish, or use in Kim Bap (p. 118-19).

Per servings: Calories: 131, Protein: 8 g, Fat: 9 g, Carbohydrates: 2 g

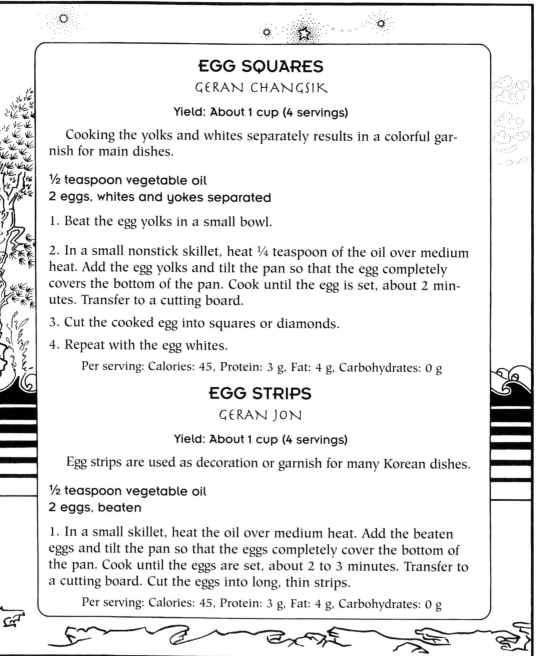

EGG SQUARES

GERAN CHANGSIK

Yield: About 1 cup (4 servings)

Cooking the yolks and whites separately results in a colorful garnish for main dishes.

½ teaspoon vegetable oil
2 eggs, whites and yokes separated

1. Beat the egg yolks in a small bowl.

2. In a small nonstick skillet, heat ¼ teaspoon of the oil over medium heat. Add the egg yolks and tilt the pan so that the egg completely covers the bottom of the pan. Cook until the egg is set, about 2 minutes. Transfer to a cutting board.

3. Cut the cooked egg into squares or diamonds.

4. Repeat with the egg whites.

Per serving: Calories: 45, Protein: 3 g, Fat: 4 g, Carbohydrates: 0 g

EGG STRIPS

GERAN JON

Yield: About 1 cup (4 servings)

Egg strips are used as decoration or garnish for many Korean dishes.

½ teaspoon vegetable oil
2 eggs, beaten

1. In a small skillet, heat the oil over medium heat. Add the beaten eggs and tilt the pan so that the eggs completely cover the bottom of the pan. Cook until the eggs are set, about 2 to 3 minutes. Transfer to a cutting board. Cut the eggs into long, thin strips.

Per serving: Calories: 45, Protein: 3 g, Fat: 4 g, Carbohydrates: 0 g

EGGPLANT TOFU

KAJI TUBU BOKUM

Yield: 2 main-dish or 4 side-dish servings

1 Japanese eggplant
1 tablespoon vegetable oil
1 pound fresh tofu, cut into bite-size cubes
1 green chili pepper, seeded and thinly sliced
4 green onions, green and white parts, cut into 1-inch pieces
2 cloves garlic, minced
2 tablespoons soy sauce
1 teaspoon rice vinegar
1 teaspoon toasted sesame seeds

1. Parboil or steam the eggplant for 5 minutes. Drain and cool. Cut the eggplant into 1-inch cubes.

2. In a wok or large skillet, heat the oil over high heat. Add the eggplant, tofu, chili pepper, onions, and garlic. Stir-fry 2 minutes.

3. Mix together the soy sauce and rice vinegar. Pour over the vegetables and cook until the moisture is absorbed, about 1 minute.

4. Transfer to a serving platter, and sprinkle with the sesame seeds before serving.

Per 3 servings: Calories: 226, Protein: 13 g, Fat: 10 g, Carbohydrates: 17 g

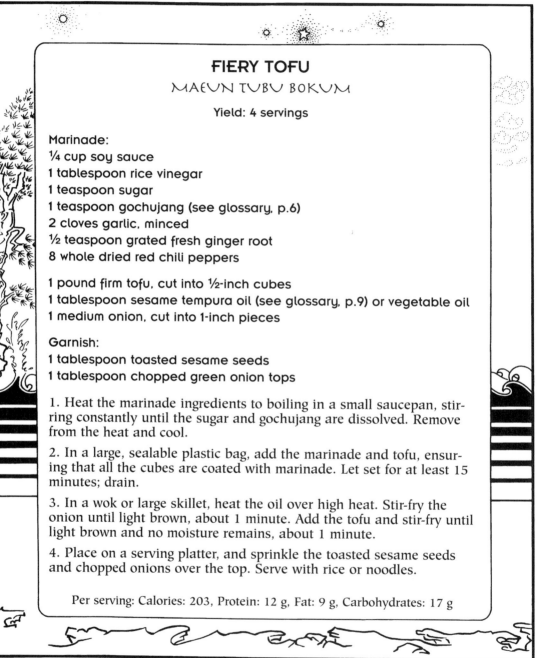

FIERY TOFU
MAEUN TUBU BOKUM

Yield: 4 servings

Marinade:
¼ cup soy sauce
1 tablespoon rice vinegar
1 teaspoon sugar
1 teaspoon gochujang (see glossary, p.6)
2 cloves garlic, minced
½ teaspoon grated fresh ginger root
8 whole dried red chili peppers

1 pound firm tofu, cut into ½-inch cubes
1 tablespoon sesame tempura oil (see glossary, p.9) or vegetable oil
1 medium onion, cut into 1-inch pieces

Garnish:
1 tablespoon toasted sesame seeds
1 tablespoon chopped green onion tops

1. Heat the marinade ingredients to boiling in a small saucepan, stirring constantly until the sugar and gochujang are dissolved. Remove from the heat and cool.

2. In a large, sealable plastic bag, add the marinade and tofu, ensuring that all the cubes are coated with marinade. Let set for at least 15 minutes; drain.

3. In a wok or large skillet, heat the oil over high heat. Stir-fry the onion until light brown, about 1 minute. Add the tofu and stir-fry until light brown and no moisture remains, about 1 minute.

4. Place on a serving platter, and sprinkle the toasted sesame seeds and chopped onions over the top. Serve with rice or noodles.

Per serving: Calories: 203, Protein: 12 g, Fat: 9 g, Carbohydrates: 17 g

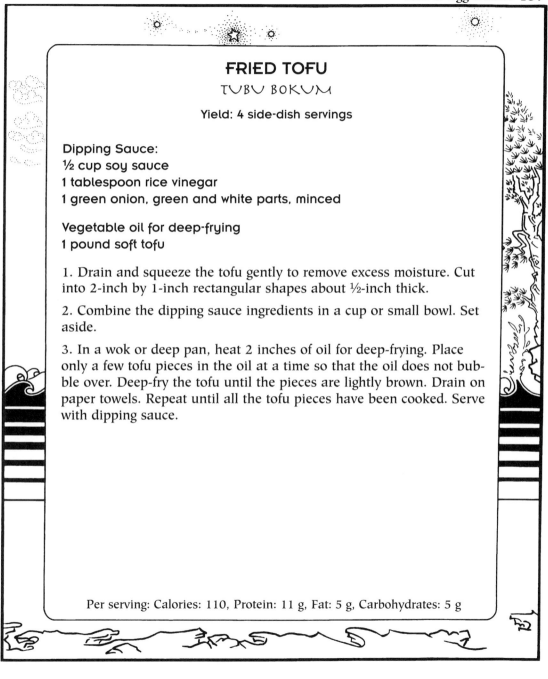

FRIED TOFU

TUBU BOKUM

Yield: 4 side-dish servings

Dipping Sauce:
½ cup soy sauce
1 tablespoon rice vinegar
1 green onion, green and white parts, minced

Vegetable oil for deep-frying
1 pound soft tofu

1. Drain and squeeze the tofu gently to remove excess moisture. Cut into 2-inch by 1-inch rectangular shapes about ½-inch thick.

2. Combine the dipping sauce ingredients in a cup or small bowl. Set aside.

3. In a wok or deep pan, heat 2 inches of oil for deep-frying. Place only a few tofu pieces in the oil at a time so that the oil does not bubble over. Deep-fry the tofu until the pieces are lightly brown. Drain on paper towels. Repeat until all the tofu pieces have been cooked. Serve with dipping sauce.

Per serving: Calories: 110, Protein: 11 g, Fat: 5 g, Carbohydrates: 5 g

GINGER TOFU

SANGKANG TUBU MUCHIM

Yield: 2 generous servings

This is another favorite tofu recipe—a gentle ginger flavor and not too spicy.

Ginger Marinade:
1 teaspoon grated fresh ginger root
3 tablespoons soy sauce
1 tablespoon rice vinegar

1 pound firm tofu, drained and cubed
1 tablespoon sesame tempura oil (see glossary, p. 9), or vegetable
   oil plus 2 or 3 drops sesame oil
2 cloves garlic, minced
4 green onions, green and white parts, chopped

1. Combine the ginger marinade ingredients in a medium bowl.

2. Add the cubes of tofu, and stir to coat. Marinate 5 minutes. Drain; discard marinade.

3. Heat the oil in a wok or large skillet. Add the garlic and onions. Stir-fry for 1 minute. Add the tofu and stir-fry until light brown. Serve warm.

Per serving: Calories: 255, Protein: 18 g, Fat: 15 g, Carbohydrates: 7 g

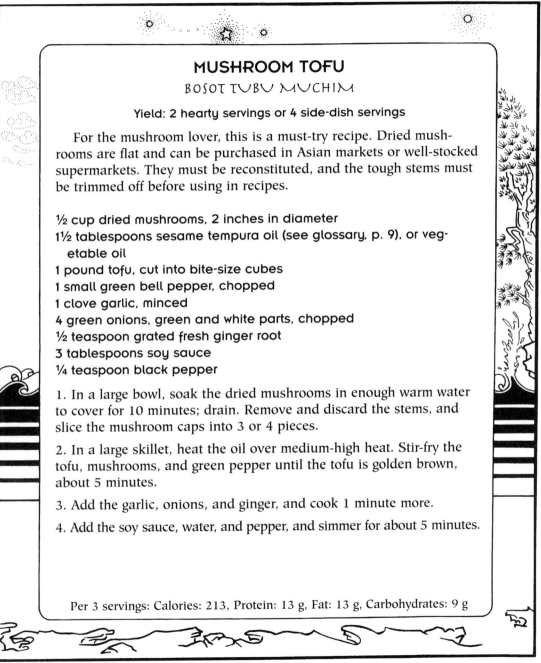

MUSHROOM TOFU

BOSOT TUBU MUCHIM

Yield: 2 hearty servings or 4 side-dish servings

For the mushroom lover, this is a must-try recipe. Dried mushrooms are flat and can be purchased in Asian markets or well-stocked supermarkets. They must be reconstituted, and the tough stems must be trimmed off before using in recipes.

½ cup dried mushrooms, 2 inches in diameter
1½ tablespoons sesame tempura oil (see glossary, p. 9), or vegetable oil
1 pound tofu, cut into bite-size cubes
1 small green bell pepper, chopped
1 clove garlic, minced
4 green onions, green and white parts, chopped
½ teaspoon grated fresh ginger root
3 tablespoons soy sauce
¼ teaspoon black pepper

1. In a large bowl, soak the dried mushrooms in enough warm water to cover for 10 minutes; drain. Remove and discard the stems, and slice the mushroom caps into 3 or 4 pieces.

2. In a large skillet, heat the oil over medium-high heat. Stir-fry the tofu, mushrooms, and green pepper until the tofu is golden brown, about 5 minutes.

3. Add the garlic, onions, and ginger, and cook 1 minute more.

4. Add the soy sauce, water, and pepper, and simmer for about 5 minutes.

Per 3 servings: Calories: 213, Protein: 13 g, Fat: 13 g, Carbohydrates: 9 g

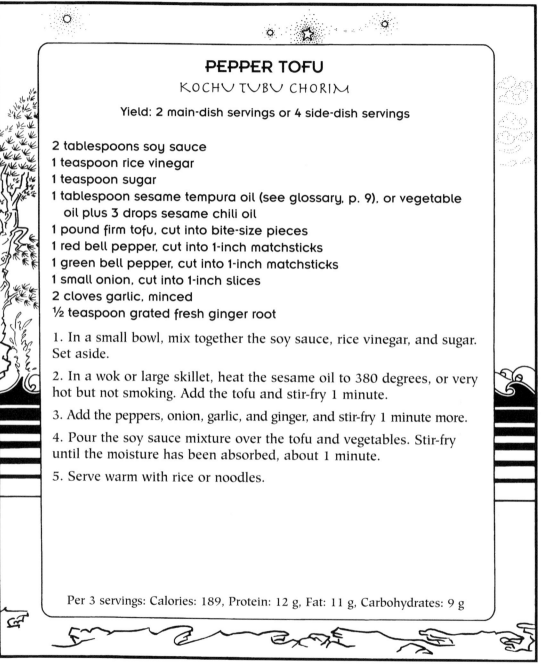

PEPPER TOFU

KOCHU TUBU CHORIM

Yield: 2 main-dish servings or 4 side-dish servings

2 tablespoons soy sauce
1 teaspoon rice vinegar
1 teaspoon sugar
1 tablespoon sesame tempura oil (see glossary, p. 9), or vegetable
   oil plus 3 drops sesame chili oil
1 pound firm tofu, cut into bite-size pieces
1 red bell pepper, cut into 1-inch matchsticks
1 green bell pepper, cut into 1-inch matchsticks
1 small onion, cut into 1-inch slices
2 cloves garlic, minced
½ teaspoon grated fresh ginger root

1. In a small bowl, mix together the soy sauce, rice vinegar, and sugar. Set aside.

2. In a wok or large skillet, heat the sesame oil to 380 degrees, or very hot but not smoking. Add the tofu and stir-fry 1 minute.

3. Add the peppers, onion, garlic, and ginger, and stir-fry 1 minute more.

4. Pour the soy sauce mixture over the tofu and vegetables. Stir-fry until the moisture has been absorbed, about 1 minute.

5. Serve warm with rice or noodles.

Per 3 servings: Calories: 189, Protein: 12 g, Fat: 11 g, Carbohydrates: 9 g

SESAME TOFU

BIBIM TUBU

Yield: 4 servings

1 pound fresh tofu, cut into about 16 rectangular pieces, 3 inches
  long by 1½ inches wide by ½ inch thick
1 teaspoon sesame salt
2 teaspoons toasted sesame seeds
¼ cup water
2 green onions, green and white parts, minced
2 cloves garlic, crushed
1 tablespoon vegetable oil
20 dried red pepper threads (see red chili pepper, p. 7)

1. Sprinkle the tofu slices with the sesame salt, and let stand for 15 minutes. Spread the toasted sesame seeds on 8 of the tofu slices. Place a plain tofu slice on each of the sesame tofu slices so that the sesame seeds are sandwiched between the tofu slices.

2. Mix together the soy sauce, water, onions, and garlic in a small bowl.

3. In a wok or large, deep pan, heat the oil over medium heat. Add 2 tablespoons of the soy sauce mixture and a few dried red chili threads into the pan.

4. Place the 8 sesame tofu "sandwiches" in the pan. Drizzle the rest of the soy sauce mixture over the tofu. Spread the rest of the chili threads on top. Cover the pan and steam until most of the liquid has been absorbed, about 15 minutes.

5. Place on a serving platter. Serve warm with rice.

Per serving: Calories: 137, Protein: 10 g, Fat: 9 g, Carbohydrates: 4 g

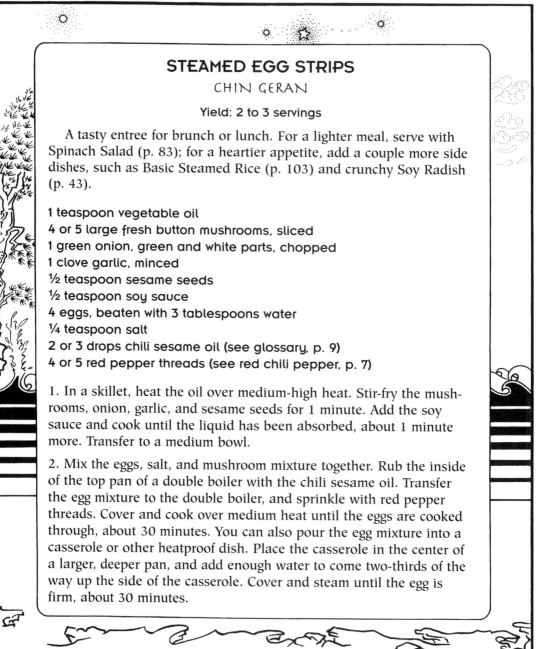

STEAMED EGG STRIPS

CHIN GERAN

Yield: 2 to 3 servings

A tasty entree for brunch or lunch. For a lighter meal, serve with Spinach Salad (p. 83); for a heartier appetite, add a couple more side dishes, such as Basic Steamed Rice (p. 103) and crunchy Soy Radish (p. 43).

1 teaspoon vegetable oil
4 or 5 large fresh button mushrooms, sliced
1 green onion, green and white parts, chopped
1 clove garlic, minced
½ teaspoon sesame seeds
½ teaspoon soy sauce
4 eggs, beaten with 3 tablespoons water
¼ teaspoon salt
2 or 3 drops chili sesame oil (see glossary, p. 9)
4 or 5 red pepper threads (see red chili pepper, p. 7)

1. In a skillet, heat the oil over medium-high heat. Stir-fry the mushrooms, onion, garlic, and sesame seeds for 1 minute. Add the soy sauce and cook until the liquid has been absorbed, about 1 minute more. Transfer to a medium bowl.

2. Mix the eggs, salt, and mushroom mixture together. Rub the inside of the top pan of a double boiler with the chili sesame oil. Transfer the egg mixture to the double boiler, and sprinkle with red pepper threads. Cover and cook over medium heat until the eggs are cooked through, about 30 minutes. You can also pour the egg mixture into a casserole or other heatproof dish. Place the casserole in the center of a larger, deeper pan, and add enough water to come two-thirds of the way up the side of the casserole. Cover and steam until the egg is firm, about 30 minutes.

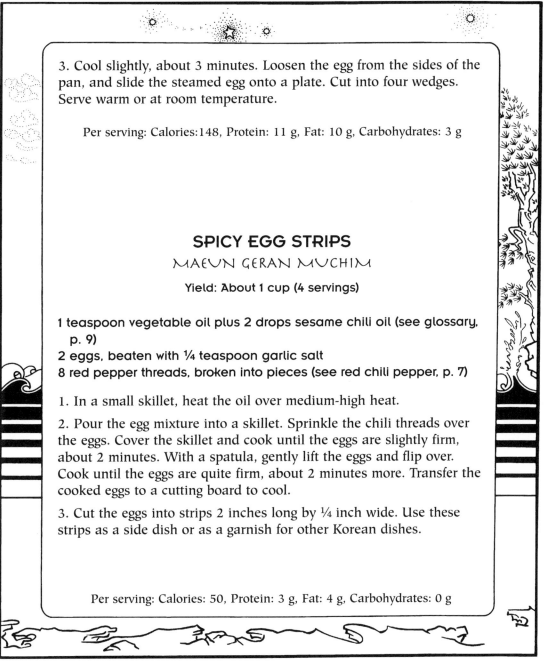

3. Cool slightly, about 3 minutes. Loosen the egg from the sides of the pan, and slide the steamed egg onto a plate. Cut into four wedges. Serve warm or at room temperature.

Per serving: Calories:148, Protein: 11 g, Fat: 10 g, Carbohydrates: 3 g

SPICY EGG STRIPS

MAEUN GERAN MUCHIM

Yield: About 1 cup (4 servings)

1 teaspoon vegetable oil plus 2 drops sesame chili oil (see glossary, p. 9)
2 eggs, beaten with ¼ teaspoon garlic salt
8 red pepper threads, broken into pieces (see red chili pepper, p. 7)

1. In a small skillet, heat the oil over medium-high heat.

2. Pour the egg mixture into a skillet. Sprinkle the chili threads over the eggs. Cover the skillet and cook until the eggs are slightly firm, about 2 minutes. With a spatula, gently lift the eggs and flip over. Cook until the eggs are quite firm, about 2 minutes more. Transfer the cooked eggs to a cutting board to cool.

3. Cut the eggs into strips 2 inches long by ¼ inch wide. Use these strips as a side dish or as a garnish for other Korean dishes.

Per serving: Calories: 50, Protein: 3 g, Fat: 4 g, Carbohydrates: 0 g

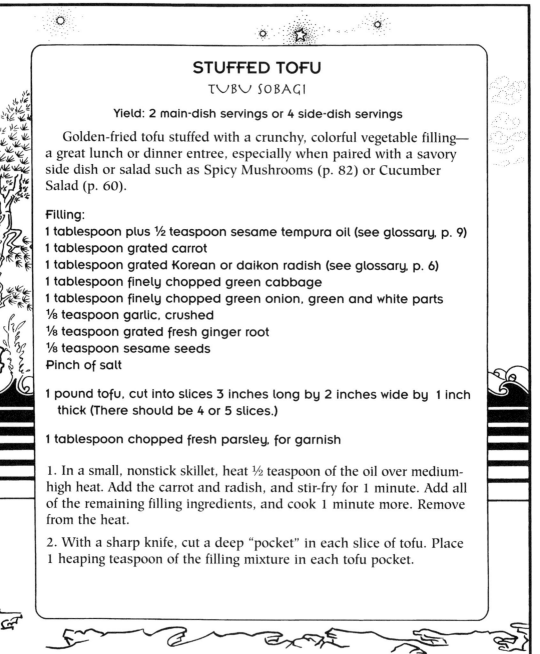

STUFFED TOFU

TUBU SOBAGI

Yield: 2 main-dish servings or 4 side-dish servings

Golden-fried tofu stuffed with a crunchy, colorful vegetable filling—a great lunch or dinner entree, especially when paired with a savory side dish or salad such as Spicy Mushrooms (p. 82) or Cucumber Salad (p. 60).

Filling:
1 tablespoon plus ½ teaspoon sesame tempura oil (see glossary, p. 9)
1 tablespoon grated carrot
1 tablespoon grated Korean or daikon radish (see glossary, p. 6)
1 tablespoon finely chopped green cabbage
1 tablespoon finely chopped green onion, green and white parts
⅛ teaspoon garlic, crushed
⅛ teaspoon grated fresh ginger root
⅛ teaspoon sesame seeds
Pinch of salt

1 pound tofu, cut into slices 3 inches long by 2 inches wide by 1 inch thick (There should be 4 or 5 slices.)

1 tablespoon chopped fresh parsley, for garnish

1. In a small, nonstick skillet, heat ½ teaspoon of the oil over medium-high heat. Add the carrot and radish, and stir-fry for 1 minute. Add all of the remaining filling ingredients, and cook 1 minute more. Remove from the heat.

2. With a sharp knife, cut a deep "pocket" in each slice of tofu. Place 1 heaping teaspoon of the filling mixture in each tofu pocket.

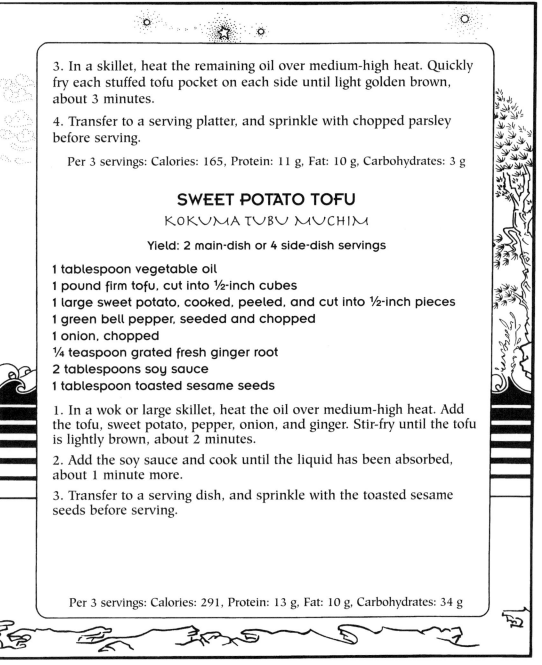

3. In a skillet, heat the remaining oil over medium-high heat. Quickly fry each stuffed tofu pocket on each side until light golden brown, about 3 minutes.

4. Transfer to a serving platter, and sprinkle with chopped parsley before serving.

Per 3 servings: Calories: 165, Protein: 11 g, Fat: 10 g, Carbohydrates: 3 g

SWEET POTATO TOFU

KOKUMA TUBU MUCHIM

Yield: 2 main-dish or 4 side-dish servings

1 tablespoon vegetable oil
1 pound firm tofu, cut into ½-inch cubes
1 large sweet potato, cooked, peeled, and cut into ½-inch pieces
1 green bell pepper, seeded and chopped
1 onion, chopped
¼ teaspoon grated fresh ginger root
2 tablespoons soy sauce
1 tablespoon toasted sesame seeds

1. In a wok or large skillet, heat the oil over medium-high heat. Add the tofu, sweet potato, pepper, onion, and ginger. Stir-fry until the tofu is lightly brown, about 2 minutes.

2. Add the soy sauce and cook until the liquid has been absorbed, about 1 minute more.

3. Transfer to a serving dish, and sprinkle with the toasted sesame seeds before serving.

Per 3 servings: Calories: 291, Protein: 13 g, Fat: 10 g, Carbohydrates: 34 g

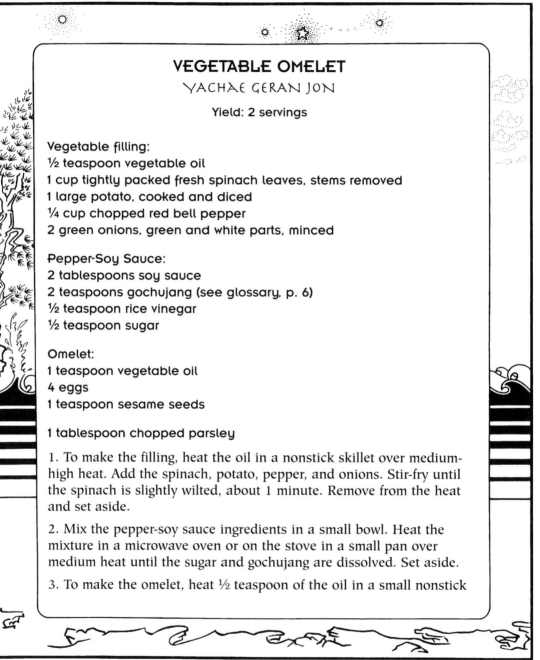

VEGETABLE OMELET

ΥΑϹΗΑΕ ϹΕRΑΝ JON

Yield: 2 servings

Vegetable filling:
½ teaspoon vegetable oil
1 cup tightly packed fresh spinach leaves, stems removed
1 large potato, cooked and diced
¼ cup chopped red bell pepper
2 green onions, green and white parts, minced

Pepper-Soy Sauce:
2 tablespoons soy sauce
2 teaspoons gochujang (see glossary, p. 6)
½ teaspoon rice vinegar
½ teaspoon sugar

Omelet:
1 teaspoon vegetable oil
4 eggs
1 teaspoon sesame seeds

1 tablespoon chopped parsley

1. To make the filling, heat the oil in a nonstick skillet over medium-high heat. Add the spinach, potato, pepper, and onions. Stir-fry until the spinach is slightly wilted, about 1 minute. Remove from the heat and set aside.

2. Mix the pepper-soy sauce ingredients in a small bowl. Heat the mixture in a microwave oven or on the stove in a small pan over medium heat until the sugar and gochujang are dissolved. Set aside.

3. To make the omelet, heat ½ teaspoon of the oil in a small nonstick

skillet or omelet pan over moderate heat. Beat 2 of the eggs in a small bowl. Sprinkle the sesame seeds in the skillet, and then pour in the beaten eggs. Tilt the pan so that the egg completely covers the bottom. Cover and cook until the eggs are set.

4. Place ½ of the spinach mixture on the bottom half of the omelet. Fold over the top half to cover the vegetables. Gently remove from the pan, and place on the serving plate. Repeat for the second omelet. Serve drizzled with the sauce, and garnished with parsley.

Per serving: Calories: 299, Protein: 17 g, Fat: 17 g, Carbohydrates: 23 g

Sweets & Desserts

In Korea, the culmination of a fine repast does not necessarily end with the rich, sugary desserts that many of us are accustomed to eating. At times, a baked dessert will be served, but it's not overly sweet or fat-laden. Usually, fresh fruit or a cool, soothing drink is presented at the end of the meal. Not only is this a simple, nutritious final course, but it also serves to neutralize the fire from the food eaten earlier in the meal.

I remember my first encounter with the deliciously mellow Ginger Drink with both fondness and humility. Young and I had justed finished a lovely meal at a popular Korean restaurant. Our server placed a small bowl of shimmering liquid in front of me. Being pathetically nearsighted, I didn't notice the pine nuts floating in the bowl. I ignorantly yet delicately proceeded to wash my fingers off in what I thought was a water finger bowl. From the shocked look Young and the waitress shot at me, you would have thought I was going to next suck the sweet dessert off my fingers! With consummate Oriental graciousness—and without so much as a giggle—Young gently explained the Korean concept of dessert. Ginger Drink should be swallowed, not wallowed in. Oh, well. I believe that was the same dinner in which I was discussing using cattails as an interesting autumn centerpiece, and Young thought it was cruel to cut off our pet cats' tails. So much for dessert and cultural exchanges!

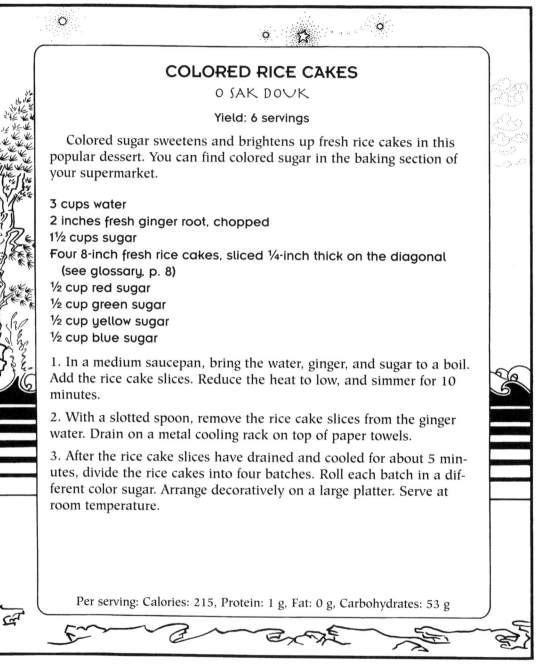

COLORED RICE CAKES

O SAK DOUK

Yield: 6 servings

Colored sugar sweetens and brightens up fresh rice cakes in this popular dessert. You can find colored sugar in the baking section of your supermarket.

3 cups water
2 inches fresh ginger root, chopped
1½ cups sugar
Four 8-inch fresh rice cakes, sliced ¼-inch thick on the diagonal
   (see glossary, p. 8)
½ cup red sugar
½ cup green sugar
½ cup yellow sugar
½ cup blue sugar

1. In a medium saucepan, bring the water, ginger, and sugar to a boil. Add the rice cake slices. Reduce the heat to low, and simmer for 10 minutes.

2. With a slotted spoon, remove the rice cake slices from the ginger water. Drain on a metal cooling rack on top of paper towels.

3. After the rice cake slices have drained and cooled for about 5 minutes, divide the rice cakes into four batches. Roll each batch in a different color sugar. Arrange decoratively on a large platter. Serve at room temperature.

Per serving: Calories: 215, Protein: 1 g, Fat: 0 g, Carbohydrates: 53 g

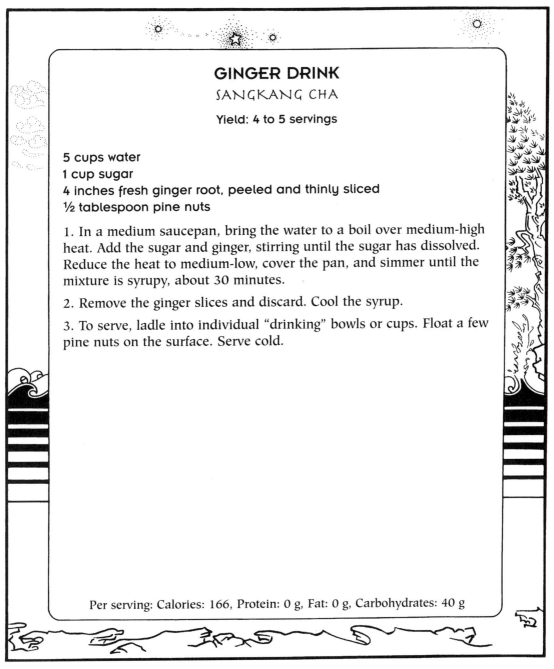

GINGER DRINK

SANGKANG CHA

Yield: 4 to 5 servings

5 cups water
1 cup sugar
4 inches fresh ginger root, peeled and thinly sliced
½ tablespoon pine nuts

1. In a medium saucepan, bring the water to a boil over medium-high heat. Add the sugar and ginger, stirring until the sugar has dissolved. Reduce the heat to medium-low, cover the pan, and simmer until the mixture is syrupy, about 30 minutes.

2. Remove the ginger slices and discard. Cool the syrup.

3. To serve, ladle into individual "drinking" bowls or cups. Float a few pine nuts on the surface. Serve cold.

Per serving: Calories: 166, Protein: 0 g, Fat: 0 g, Carbohydrates: 40 g

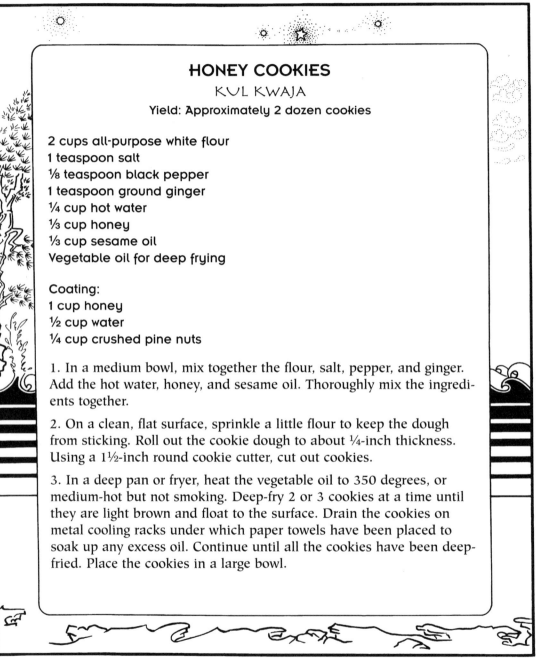

HONEY COOKIES
KUL KWAJA
Yield: Approximately 2 dozen cookies

2 cups all-purpose white flour
1 teaspoon salt
⅛ teaspoon black pepper
1 teaspoon ground ginger
¼ cup hot water
⅓ cup honey
⅓ cup sesame oil
Vegetable oil for deep frying

Coating:
1 cup honey
½ cup water
¼ cup crushed pine nuts

1. In a medium bowl, mix together the flour, salt, pepper, and ginger. Add the hot water, honey, and sesame oil. Thoroughly mix the ingredients together.

2. On a clean, flat surface, sprinkle a little flour to keep the dough from sticking. Roll out the cookie dough to about ¼-inch thickness. Using a 1½-inch round cookie cutter, cut out cookies.

3. In a deep pan or fryer, heat the vegetable oil to 350 degrees, or medium-hot but not smoking. Deep-fry 2 or 3 cookies at a time until they are light brown and float to the surface. Drain the cookies on metal cooling racks under which paper towels have been placed to soak up any excess oil. Continue until all the cookies have been deep-fried. Place the cookies in a large bowl.

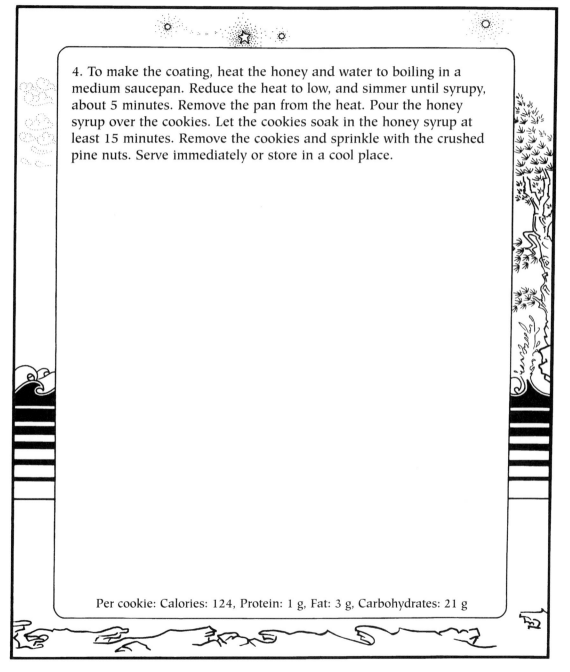

4. To make the coating, heat the honey and water to boiling in a medium saucepan. Reduce the heat to low, and simmer until syrupy, about 5 minutes. Remove the pan from the heat. Pour the honey syrup over the cookies. Let the cookies soak in the honey syrup at least 15 minutes. Remove the cookies and sprinkle with the crushed pine nuts. Serve immediately or store in a cool place.

Per cookie: Calories: 124, Protein: 1 g, Fat: 3 g, Carbohydrates: 21 g

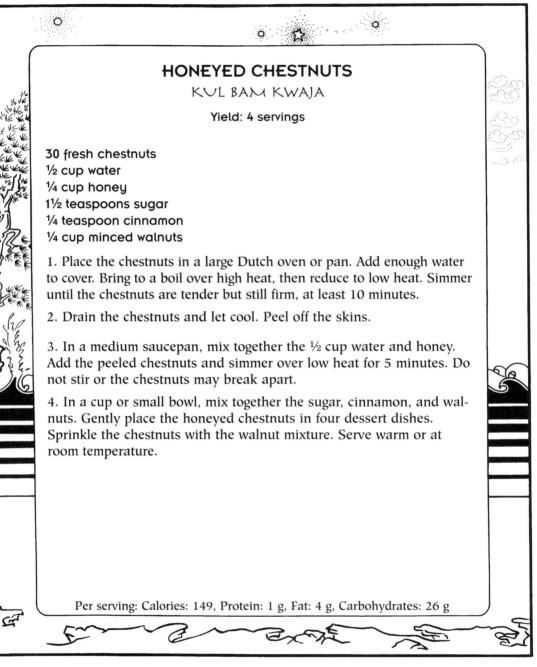

HONEYED CHESTNUTS

KUL BAM KWAJA

Yield: 4 servings

30 fresh chestnuts
½ cup water
¼ cup honey
1½ teaspoons sugar
¼ teaspoon cinnamon
¼ cup minced walnuts

1. Place the chestnuts in a large Dutch oven or pan. Add enough water to cover. Bring to a boil over high heat, then reduce to low heat. Simmer until the chestnuts are tender but still firm, at least 10 minutes.

2. Drain the chestnuts and let cool. Peel off the skins.

3. In a medium saucepan, mix together the ½ cup water and honey. Add the peeled chestnuts and simmer over low heat for 5 minutes. Do not stir or the chestnuts may break apart.

4. In a cup or small bowl, mix together the sugar, cinnamon, and walnuts. Gently place the honeyed chestnuts in four dessert dishes. Sprinkle the chestnuts with the walnut mixture. Serve warm or at room temperature.

Per serving: Calories: 149, Protein: 1 g, Fat: 4 g, Carbohydrates: 26 g

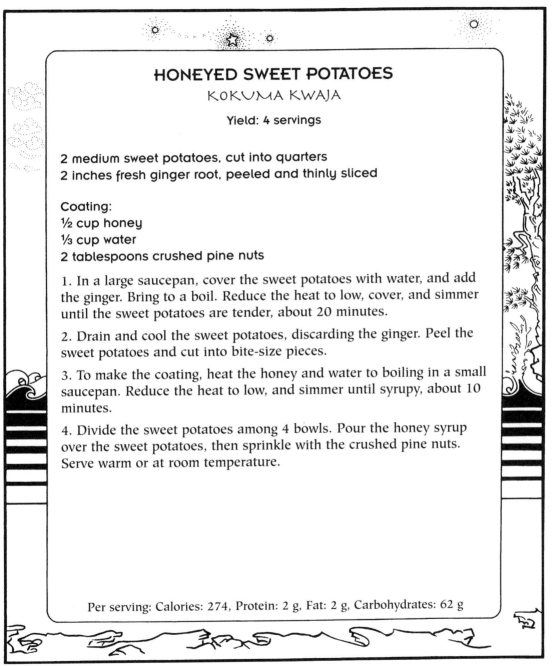

HONEYED SWEET POTATOES

KOKUMA KWAJA

Yield: 4 servings

2 medium sweet potatoes, cut into quarters
2 inches fresh ginger root, peeled and thinly sliced

Coating:
½ cup honey
⅓ cup water
2 tablespoons crushed pine nuts

1. In a large saucepan, cover the sweet potatoes with water, and add the ginger. Bring to a boil. Reduce the heat to low, cover, and simmer until the sweet potatoes are tender, about 20 minutes.

2. Drain and cool the sweet potatoes, discarding the ginger. Peel the sweet potatoes and cut into bite-size pieces.

3. To make the coating, heat the honey and water to boiling in a small saucepan. Reduce the heat to low, and simmer until syrupy, about 10 minutes.

4. Divide the sweet potatoes among 4 bowls. Pour the honey syrup over the sweet potatoes, then sprinkle with the crushed pine nuts. Serve warm or at room temperature.

Per serving: Calories: 274, Protein: 2 g, Fat: 2 g, Carbohydrates: 62 g

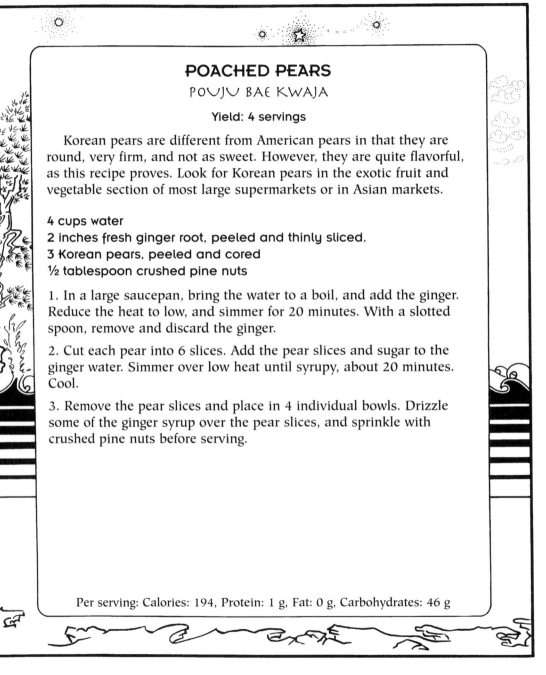

POACHED PEARS
POUJU BAE KWAJA

Yield: 4 servings

Korean pears are different from American pears in that they are round, very firm, and not as sweet. However, they are quite flavorful, as this recipe proves. Look for Korean pears in the exotic fruit and vegetable section of most large supermarkets or in Asian markets.

4 cups water
2 inches fresh ginger root, peeled and thinly sliced.
3 Korean pears, peeled and cored
½ tablespoon crushed pine nuts

1. In a large saucepan, bring the water to a boil, and add the ginger. Reduce the heat to low, and simmer for 20 minutes. With a slotted spoon, remove and discard the ginger.

2. Cut each pear into 6 slices. Add the pear slices and sugar to the ginger water. Simmer over low heat until syrupy, about 20 minutes. Cool.

3. Remove the pear slices and place in 4 individual bowls. Drizzle some of the ginger syrup over the pear slices, and sprinkle with crushed pine nuts before serving.

Per serving: Calories: 194, Protein: 1 g, Fat: 0 g, Carbohydrates: 46 g

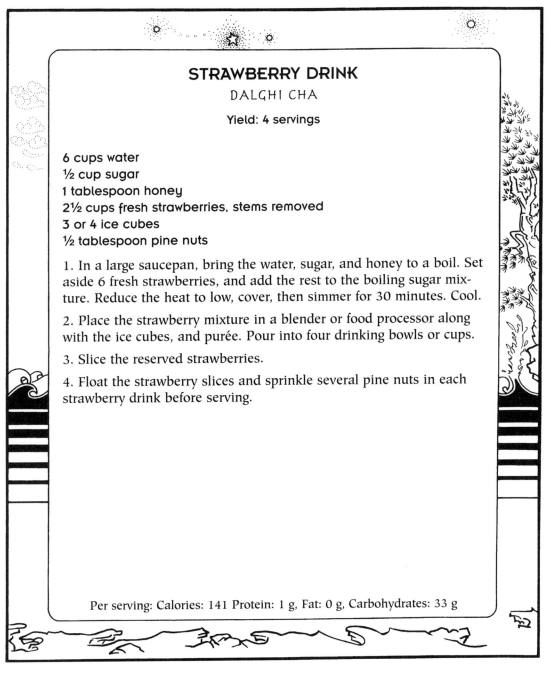

STRAWBERRY DRINK

DALGHI CHA

Yield: 4 servings

6 cups water
½ cup sugar
1 tablespoon honey
2½ cups fresh strawberries, stems removed
3 or 4 ice cubes
½ tablespoon pine nuts

1. In a large saucepan, bring the water, sugar, and honey to a boil. Set aside 6 fresh strawberries, and add the rest to the boiling sugar mixture. Reduce the heat to low, cover, then simmer for 30 minutes. Cool.

2. Place the strawberry mixture in a blender or food processor along with the ice cubes, and purée. Pour into four drinking bowls or cups.

3. Slice the reserved strawberries.

4. Float the strawberry slices and sprinkle several pine nuts in each strawberry drink before serving.

Per serving: Calories: 141 Protein: 1 g, Fat: 0 g, Carbohydrates: 33 g

MENU SUGGESTIONS

A typical Korean dinner is generally comprised of a soup, at least one kimchi dish, several side dishes, a main dish, and a sweet drink or fresh fruit to clean and cool the palate. This is the type of meal that would be served in the home of a gracious host or hostess or in a Korean restaurant. The emphasis is on a variety of foods rather than on a large quantity of any one dish. Fortunately, breakfast and lunch don't require as many different dishes. And lest this cooking task sounds daunting, remember that most kimchis and side dishes can and should be prepared a day or two ahead of time to allow the flavors to blend.

Many Korean recipes require chopped, sliced, or shredded ingredients. By having these ingredients already prepared and all other ingredients listed in the recipe in the general cooking area, the cooking process will be much easier. This is especially important if you are preparing dishes that must be cooked immediately prior to serving to ensure crispness and/or flavor. Try not to have too many last-minute dishes on your menu. There are main dishes such as fried rice that can be prepared ahead of time and kept warm in the oven. Remember, you also want to enjoy this meal and not be slaving away in a hot kitchen while your guests are dining.

Flavor and aesthetics should also be taken into consideration when planning a Korean menu. Since many Korean dishes are quite spicy, it would behoove the considerate cook to include one or two less zesty dishes for balance. A mild soup, such as Radish Soup, at the beginning of the meal and a cool dessert, such as Ginger Drink, ending the meal are two such culinary "bookends" that would counterbalance a spicy main course. And the table arrangement of these various foods is such an easy task: kimchis and side dishes are served in small bowls conveniently placed down the center of the table so that all diners have easy access to them. The various colors and textures of the dishes are not only pleasing to the eye but to the palate as well.

Trying new recipes can be an exciting adventure. But it can also be intimidating. In this last chapter, we have provided some sample menus to be used as guidelines. Hopefully, as you become more confident in using these recipes, you will attempt to mix and match flavor combinations according to your own taste. And if there is one thing of which you can be sure, it's that no matter what combination of foods you choose to try, there is nothing boring about Korean cuisine.

BRUNCH FOR SIX

Rice Balls 112-13
Vegetable Omelet 168-69
Sweet Potato Pancakes 89
Cabbage Noodle Salad 59
Sesame Mushrooms 76
Honey Cookies 174-75
Strawberry Drink 179

SPRING LUNCH FOR FOUR

Spinach Soup 29
Basic Steamed Rice 103
Stuffed Lettuce Rolls 86-87
Mushroom Noodles 1388
Ginger Drink 173

SUMMER LUNCH FOR FOUR

Spinach Salad 83
Cucumber Noodles 130
Basic Steamed Rice 103
Spicy Bean Sprouts 80
Tofu Cubes 152
fresh fruit

AUTUMN LUNCH FOR FOUR

Bean Paste and Tofu Soup 13
Basic Steamed Rice 103
Cabbage Radish Pickle 37
Spicy Mushrooms 37
Fried Red Pepper Potatoes 65
Ginger Drink 173

WINTER LUNCH FOR FOUR

Noodle Soup 22
Basic Steamed Rice 103
Cabbage Pickle 36
Red Pepper Broccoli 72
Sesame Tofu 163
Steamed Egg Strips 164-65
Honey Cookies 174-75

LIGHT LOW-FAT LUNCH

Radish Soup 25
Rice with Mixed Vegetables 116
Cucumber Salad 60
Spicy Bean Sprouts 80
Turnip Salad 92
fresh fruit

CLEAR-THE-STUFFY-HEAD LUNCH

Kimchi Soup 20
Basic Steamed Rice 103
Egg Squares 156
Sesame Seaweed Squares 78
hot tea

PICNIC FOR FOUR

Seaweed Rice Rolls 118
sweet Korean (daikon) radish
Sesame Spinach 79
Marinated Black Beans 57
hard-boiled eggs
Bean Sprout Pancakes 54-55
Ginger Drink 173
fresh fruit

DINNER FOR FOUR

Dumpling Soup 18
Stuffed Cabbage Pickle 44-45
Turnip Salad 92
Soy Radish 43
Spicy Bean Sprouts 80
Sesame Spinach 79
Barbecued Tofu 151
Basic Steamed Rice 103
Sesame Seaweed Squares 78
Strawberry Drink 179

PYROMANIAC'S DREAM DINNER FOR FOUR (FIERY HOT)

Bean Sprout Soup 14
Fiery Fried Rice 108
Eggplant Pickle 41
Fried Kimchi Eggrolls 136-37
Hot Pepper Noodles 135
Fiery Tofu 158
Poached Pears 178
pitcher of ice water

SUMMER SUPPER FOR FOUR

Cold Noodle Salad 128-29
Basic Steamed Rice 103
Sesame Seaweed Squares 788
Barbecued Tofu 151
Green Onion Pickle 42
Marinated Black Beans 57
Fried Green Peppers 64
Ginger Drink 73

VEGETARIAN BARBECUE FOR FOUR TO SIX

Mild Fried Rice 107
Spinach Salad 83
Cucumber Pickle 38
Eggplant Pickle 41
Marinated Black Beans 57
Grilled Vegetables 66-67
Barbecued Tofu 151
Honey Cookies 174-75
Ginger Drink 173

DINNER PARTY FOR SIX TO EIGHT

Vegetable Salad with Sesame Dressing 98-99
Basic Steamed Rice 103
Sesame Seaweed Squares 78
Steamed Egg Strips 164-65
Green Onion Pickle 42
Cabbage Pickle 36
Sesame Spinach 79
Spicy Bean Sprouts 80
Soy Radish 43
Stuffed Tofu 166
Young's or Deb's Vegetable Noodles 142-45
Strawberry Drink 179

PARTY BUFFET FOR 10 TO 15

Seaweed Rice Rolls 118
Basic Steamed Rice 103
Crispy Seaweed 61
Stuffed Cabbage Pickle 44-45
Young Radish Pickle 40
Eggplant Salad 63
Vegetable Bundles 94-95
Fried Kimchi Eggrolls 136-37
Steamed Dumplings 148
Batter-Fried Sesame or Spicy Vegetables 50-53
Ginger Tofu 160
Honeyed Chestnuts 176
Colored Rice Cakes 172
Ginger Drink 173

INDEX